Chandlings 1

Get Cooking

Thor Gilje 9

Clare Walsh

Published by:
Chandlings Manor School, Oxford

Designed and typeset by:
Laura Skipper

Printed by:
Information Press, Eynsham, Oxford, OX29 4JB

Front and back cover illustrations by:
Robert Walsh

Illustrations throughout the book by:
Children of Chandlings Manor School

Author:
Clare Walsh

ISBN 0-9550067-0-8

This is for you, Chris.

All proceeds from the sale of this book will be donated to cancer research to enable scientists to continue their vital work, in researching the causes, treatment and prevention of cancer.

Notes about the recipes

✓ I use a hard vegetable margarine for making cakes, but you can substitute butter. Don't use low fat spreads for baking.

✓ Use medium fresh eggs unless stated.

✓ Soya milk can be substituted for cow's milk in any of the recipes.

✓ Cooking times do vary according to your cooker, adjust as necessary.

✓ Most recipes serve four people unless indicated.

✓ tablespoon = one 15 ml spoon.

✓ teaspoon = one 5 ml spoon.

Cooking with children

- Make it fun!

- Let children help prepare normal family meals and let them watch you cook and prepare food.

- Involve the children in growing a few vegetables or visit a pick your own or farmers markets to buy seasonal local vegetables and fruit.

- Don't mind a bit of mess (and remember that young children also love washing up!).

- Don't stop children using sharp knives and hobs, just teach them how to use them safely and be there to help.

- Teach children the importance of food hygiene and safety from an early age and insist on clean hands.

- Enjoy sharing the results.

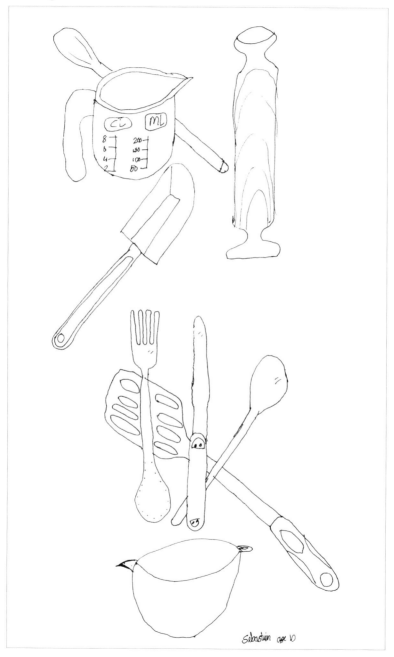

Sebastien age 10

Contents

Introduction

This book is a collection of simple, tried and tested recipes I have used as a teacher and a Mum over many years. The book was inspired by the children of Chandlings Manor School who love cooking at school and wanted more recipes they could make at home with their families. Some of the recipes can be cooked by children with very little help, but most are designed to be made together as a family, having fun chopping, talking, stirring, cooking and tasting real food.

Children love cooking, and as parents and teachers we need to encourage and develop this enthusiasm. It is never too early for children to start enjoying food and learning basic skills. From a very early age they can sit with you in the kitchen and help wash vegetables, stir cake mixtures, weigh ingredients and roll pastry, it might create a little more mess and take slightly longer, but if a child helps prepare a meal, they will be eager to eat it, and more willing to try new foods.

Many recipes in this book make the most of our superb local produce; the fresh vegetables and fruit form a vital part of a healthy diet for children and adults, and if we teach the children basic practical skills they will be able to create exciting, healthy dishes with confidence.

At Chandlings we have recently involved the children in planting and growing some organic vegetables, salads and herbs. Growing our own produce gives the children a better understanding of seasonal cycles. We will enjoy picking the vegetables, salads, herbs and fruit to use in soups, sauces, salads and crumbles.

Cooking is all about having fun, and I make no apologies for including lots of favourite cake and biscuit recipes. Making fairy cakes and crumbles are my first memories of cooking as a young child and I still love being in the kitchen and making cakes, pastry, puddings and pies for my family. Baking also teaches the child a huge amount about weighing ingredients and following recipes accurately and for many children a batch of fairy cakes or cookies will be the first recipe they cook on their own, and that is a memorable moment.

Take a little time to cook the recipes together, make it fun and enjoy sharing the results.

Happy cooking!

Clare Walsh
Head of Food Technology
Chandlings Manor School

Quick conversions

25g	=	1 oz
50g	=	2 oz
75g	=	3 oz
100g	=	4 oz
150g	=	6 oz
200g	=	8oz
450g	=	1 lb
1 kg	=	2 lb
¼ pt	=	150ml
½ pt	=	300ml
1 pt	=	600ml

Handy measures

1 rounded tablespoon of flour	=	25g
1 level tablespoon of sugar	=	25g
1 level tablespoon of syrup	=	50g
1 mug = Approx. 300ml/½pt		

A pple cake is a wonderful cake to make and is just as nice hot or cold. It is good with firm eating apples but could also be made with cooking apples.

Apple cake

300g SR flour
1 teaspoon of ground cinnamon
250g soft brown sugar
100g raisins
125g melted butter or margarine
2 large eggs, beaten
170ml milk
4 dessert apples, peeled, cored and chopped
1 red skinned apple, thinly sliced
honey to brush over

- Put the flour and cinnamon into a bowl and stir in the sugar and raisins.
- Mix in the melted butter, eggs, milk and apples and beat until smooth.
- Turn into a lined 20 cm square cake tin, or rectangular tin approximately 26 cm x 22 cm.
- Arrange the thinly sliced apple on top of the cake mixture.
- Bake for 50 minutes - 1 hour at 180 C Gas 4.
- When it is cooked brush with a little honey.
- Either eat the cake hot, with ice cream or custard or allow to cool and eat as a cake.

Because apple cakes are quite moist, they do not keep well, so store in the fridge or freeze until needed.

Apple muffins are delicious warm or cold and are really useful for lunchboxes and after school snacks. They are also lower in fat and sugar than many bought cakes and freeze well.

Apple muffins makes 12

150g SR flour
100g margarine
100g sugar
1 cooking apple - grated
2 eggs
a little water or milk if needed

Edmund 5L 10

- Put flour and margarine in the bowl.
- Rub in with your fingers to give a crumbly mixture.
- Stir in sugar and grated apple.
- Add the eggs and beat well. If the mixture is a little stiff add a little water or milk.
- Place spoonfuls into 12 paper cases.
- Bake for 15 - 20 minutes 200 C Gas 6.

You could add cinnamon to the mixture or try using brown sugar. The consistency will depend on the size of your apple and egg; it should be quite a soft dropping consistency.

William Cronk
Age 10

Apple crumble is such a lovely, easy pudding for children to make and can be enjoyed all year round but is particularly good in Autumn with fresh cooking apples, and a few blackberries to add colour.

Apple crumble serves 4 - 6

200g flour
100g butter or margarine
100g caster sugar
4 cooking apples
sugar to taste

or use: plums, blackberry and apple, raspberry and apple, damsons, rhubarb, mixed summer fruits, gooseberries.

- Put the prepared fruit in an ovenproof dish and add sugar to taste.
- Put flour, sugar and margarine into a mixing bowl. Use your fingers to rub in until you get a crumbly mixture.
- Sprinkle the crumble over the fruit.
- Bake for approx. 30 - 40 minutes at 200 C Gas 6. The exact time depends on the type of fruit used, and also the size of the dish. I find that rhubarb and gooseberry crumbles really benefit from long cooking and I normally allow an hour to get a really good result.

When you are rubbing fat into flour, make sure your hands are nice and cool, or your mixture will get sticky.

6

A sparagus risotto is a simple but beautiful dish, making the most, in early Summer, of the freshly picked British asparagus which has such an amazing flavour.

Asparagus risotto

500g British asparagus
1 onion, finely chopped
vegetable oil or butter
300g Arborio rice
750 ml hot vegetable stock
50g freshly grated parmesan
freshly ground black pepper

By David stewart
Age 9

- Gently fry the onion in a little oil or butter until it is softened.
- Add the rice and stir over a gentle heat for a couple of minutes.
- Add one ladle full of hot stock at a time and continue stirring until all the stock has been absorbed.
- Steam the asparagus for 5 minutes or until tender. (I normally cook them in a tall saucepan and cover it with a foil hat so that the stems are in water and the tips steam.)
- Cut each spear into three pieces.
- Stir the parmesan, black pepper and asparagus into the risotto and serve immediately.

I love to serve this risotto with a peppery green salad or roasted tomatoes; it is also wonderful with grilled fish.

A pricot loaf is a lovely fruity tasting cake, and is perfect as a mid morning snack with a big cup of coffee.

Apricot loaf

100g dried apricots, chopped roughly
100g raisins
1 large orange
250g SR flour
150g margarine or butter
2 large eggs, beaten
50g walnuts, chopped
150g brown sugar

Alex Grantham
Age 8

- Remove the zest from the orange and squeeze the juice into a bowl.
- Add the chopped apricots, and raisins.
- Put the flour in a bowl and rub in the margarine.
- Add the brown sugar and walnuts.
- Beat in the eggs and the dried fruit and orange mixture.
- Beat the mixture well.
- Line a large loaf tin (30 cm x 10 cm) with baking paper and pour the mixture in.
- Bake for approximately 1 hour 180 C Gas 4 until firm to touch.

Try substituting wholemeal self raising flour.

A vocado and bacon salad makes a great light meal, particularly with some interesting bread such as ciabatta or focaccia. When you make a simple salad, the quality of each ingredient is so important, which is why this is particularly nice in Summer when you can buy locally grown crisp lettuce and tomatoes that are really fresh and vine ripened.

Avocado and bacon salad serves 4

1 fresh crisp lettuce
1 bunch of spring onions
4 - 6 ripe tomatoes
2 ripe avocados
200g smoked bacon or pancetta
4 tablespoons olive oil
2 tablespoons white wine vinegar
salt and pepper
1 clove of garlic
a handful of walnuts

- Put the olive oil, wine vinegar, salt, pepper and roughly chopped garlic into the salad bowl.
- Crush the garlic with the other dressing ingredients and mix until well blended.
- Cut the spring onions into 2 cm lengths and add to the dressing.
- Cut the tomatoes into quarters and add to the dressing.
- Grill the bacon slices until crispy.
- Wash and dry the lettuce and toss in the dressing.
- Peel and slice the avocados and add to the lettuce.
- Cut the bacon slices in half and add to the salad bowl.

- Toss everything together, sprinkle over the walnuts and eat straight away whilst the bacon is still warm.

This recipe can be varied so easily according to what is in season. I add some French beans when they are available locally, asparagus is gorgeous when in season, rocket or watercress gives a good peppery taste, or put some fresh herbs in the dressing. Look out in farm shops and farmers markets for good fresh local produce.

Harriet Budgett 7

B anana and nut teabread is a low fat cake which makes excellent use of slightly too squishy bananas and is lovely spread with butter or jam. As it is low fat, it does not keep well so is better eaten fresh or freeze until needed.

Banana and nut loaf

250g SR flour
pinch of cinnamon
125g butter or margarine
125g soft brown sugar
2 large eggs
2 large bananas, mashed
75g walnut pieces

- Put the margarine and sugar in a bowl and beat together until creamy.
- Add the eggs and beat well.
- Add the bananas and walnuts and stir in.
- Using a tablespoon, stir in the flour thoroughly.
- Grease and line a 1 kg loaf tin with baking paper and spoon the mixture into it.
- Cook for 1 hour at 180 C Gas 4.
- Serve sliced and buttered.

If you prefer not to use nuts, substitute some dried fruit, cherries or coconut instead.

Anastasia Robinson
age 10

11

B iscuits are great fun to make and there are so many different types. If you are making them with children, the easiest recipe is more of a cookie where the mixture is dropped onto a baking tray or rolled in oats. Feel free to experiment with variations - add cocoa powder for chocolate ones, cherries, lemon rind, coconut or dried fruit.

Basic biscuits makes 16

100g margarine
100g caster sugar
1 egg
175g SR flour
50g rolled oats

- Put margarine and sugar into a bowl and beat together until creamy.
- Beat in the egg, then the flour to form a stiff dough.
- Flour your hands and roll the mixture into approx. 16 balls.
- Roll the balls in oats and place on two baking trays.
- Flatten each one slightly with a fork.
- Bake for 20 minutes 180 C Gas 4.
- Remove from the baking tray when the biscuits are still warm.

Allow room between the biscuits because they will spread a little.

Beefburgers are often regarded as junk food but if you choose good quality beef from a butcher who will mince it in front of you, add fresh herbs and season well, they are delicious, nutritious and the best 'fast food'. Almost as important as the beef burger are good rolls in which to serve them in. I make a basic dough with some sun dried tomato paste added.

Beef burgers

450g lean minced beef
2 cloves of garlic
fresh or dried herbs
salt and freshly ground black pepper

- Put the garlic, salt, pepper and some fresh herbs eg thyme, oregano or dried mixed herbs in a bowl and crush them all together.
- Add the minced beef and blend together, using a fork or your hands.
- Shape into eight beef burgers, approximately the same shape and size so that they cook evenly.
- Cook under a hot grill for 10 minutes, turning once.

Take care with hygiene when handling raw meat, always use a separate board.

Caroline Viney age 10

13

B olognaise sauce is so versatile, an ideal recipe to make in bulk and freeze. It can then be turned into chilli con carne, or used as a base for a shepherds pie or lasagne.

Bolognaise sauce serves 4

1 tbsp vegetable oil
1 onion finely chopped
2 garlic cloves
450g lean minced beef
2 x 400g cans chopped tomatoes
salt and pepper
dried mixed herbs

- Heat the oil in a large saucepan and fry the onion gently until golden and soft, add the garlic and soften.
- Add the mince and stir over a medium heat until it is brown, not pink.
- Add the tomatoes, 1 teaspoon of herbs and the salt and pepper.
- Bring to the boil, then turn down and simmer gently for 1 hour until the sauce is reduced, stirring occasionally.

Fresh basil added just before serving makes it smell wonderful and really enhances the flavour.

B read and butter pudding is such a traditionally British pudding, just right for Autumn and Winter meals. It is quick and easy to prepare and great for children to make. Have fun making up variations, add lemon or orange rind, use currant bread, vary the type of milk or replace the butter with apricot jam.

Bread and butter pudding serves 4

4 - 6 slices of bread
30g butter
500 ml milk
2 large eggs
30g sugar
50g raisins
a little grated nutmeg

- Butter the bread and cut into quarters.
- Arrange the bread in an ovenproof dish.
- Sprinkle the raisins and sugar over the bread.
- Break eggs into a bowl, add the milk and whisk together.
- Pour over the bread.
- Grate some nutmeg over the top.
- Cook for 30 - 40 minutes 180 C Gas 4.

Try to use good fresh eggs for this pudding.

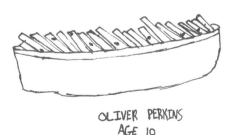

OLIVER PERKINS
AGE 10

B read rolls are such lovely things to make, all children enjoy handling and shaping the dough and getting flour everywhere! There is nothing better than the smell and taste of freshly baked bread.

Bread rolls makes 6

225g strong plain flour
half a teaspoon of salt
1 teaspoon of oil
1 packet of yeast
150 ml of warm water

- Weigh the flour then put it into the bowl.
- Add salt, oil, and yeast.
- Measure 150ml warm water.
- Pour onto the other ingredients.
- Use a fork to mix the dough together.
- Use your judgement - add a little more flour if the dough is too sticky or a little more water if it is too dry.
- Flour the table well and turn the mixture out, knead well.
- Shape into six rolls.
- Leave to rise in a warm place for 1 hour.
- Cook for 15 minutes 200 C Gas 6.

The dough is better if it is a bit sticky, just flour your hands well when kneading.

16

C aribbean fruit punch is a wonderful summer drink. It is refreshing and uses lots of fresh citrus fruit, high in Vitamin C.

Caribbean fruit punch

150g sugar
150ml water
4 large oranges
2 lemons
2 pink grapefruit
1 large mango
1 litre of soda water
lemon or lime slices and mint leaves to serve

Sammy 7

- Place the sugar and water in a pan and heat to dissolve the sugar, then leave to cool.
- Juice all the fruit and strain into a jug.
- Cut the flesh off the mango and puree using a liquidiser or hand held blender.
- Add the sugar syrup and mango to the fruit juices and stir well to combine.
- Top up the jug with the soda water and pour into your glass.
- Decorate glasses with lemon or lime and fresh mint.

Try adding passion fruit or lychees - delicious!

C hicken is such a versatile meat and this recipe could not be easier. Be imaginative with the herbs, try rosemary or basil instead of the thyme. Alternatively add some other vegetables to your parcel, asparagus is delicious in season. Try it with the couscous on p 69.

Chicken parcels serves 4

4 chicken breasts without skin
250g mixed mushrooms
olive oil
4 cloves of garlic
fresh thyme or tarragon
1 lemon
salt and pepper

- Wipe the mushrooms and slice.
- Use a piece of strong foil for each chicken breast and place the chicken in the middle.
- Rub in some olive oil and plenty of salt and pepper and garlic slivers.
- Cut some thin slices of lemon and place on top of the chicken with the thyme and mushrooms.
- Fold the foil to make a loose parcel.
- Cook for 40 minutes 180 C Gas 4.

Try adding a splash of wine to the parcel!

C helsea buns are one of my family's favourites! Like most buns they are best eaten really fresh - they are not difficult to make and if you make your own, you can add as much fruit as you like and make them as big or small as you need.

If you have a bread maker, use the same recipe and use the dough setting.

Chelsea buns makes 9

Dough
450g strong plain flour
1 teaspoon salt
2 tablespoons sugar
50g margarine
1 packet dried yeast
300ml water

Filling
25g margarine
50g caster sugar
100g dried fruit
1 teaspoon mixed spice

- Make the dough either using a bread maker or follow instructions for basic bread p 16.
- Roll the dough out to a rectangle roughly 40 x 30 cm on a floured surface.
- Melt the margarine and brush over the dough.
- Sprinkle over the dried fruit, sugar and spice.
- Roll up from the widest side and dampen the edges with water to seal.
- Cut into 9 slices and place on a baking tray, cut side facing up about 1 cm apart.

- Leave to rise in warm place for 1 hour.
- Bake in a hot oven Gas 6 200 C 25 - 30 minutes.
- Sprinkle with sugar and leave to cool on a cooling rack.

Don't worry if they have all stuck together-
they are supposed to!

by Hugo Glass, age 10

C hris' chocolate cake is a special cake, for a special person. This is a much smaller one than the one I used to make for my husband's birthday (an 18 egg mixture!). It is a really delicious cake, at its best freshly made with the chocolate still slightly warm and very gooey.

Chris' Chocolate cake

50g good cocoa powder
200 ml boiling water
175g SR flour
125g butter or margarine
300g caster sugar
2 large eggs

Filling and topping
150g plain chocolate (I use 72 % cocoa solids)
150ml soured cream

- Blend the cocoa powder with the boiling water until there are no lumps, leave to cool slightly.
- Cream the fat and sugar together with 3 tablespoons of the cocoa mixture.
- Beat in the eggs.
- Fold in the flour with the remainder of the cocoa mixture.
- Beat the mixture well, either by hand or by using a hand mixer.
- Put a circle of baking paper in the bottom of two 20 cm cake tins.
- Divide the mixture between the two tins.
- Cook for 25 - 30 minutes 180 C Gas 4.
- Turn the cooked cakes out onto a cooling rack and leave the cakes to cool.

- To make the icing, break the chocolate into pieces and put in a bowl, either pop it into the microwave for 2 minutes (stirring half way through) or place the bowl over a saucepan of boiling water and leave to melt, stirring occasionally.
- As soon as the chocolate has melted, stir in the soured cream and beat thoroughly. (You need to add the cream and beat quickly because the cold cream makes the chocolate set, and if you are a bit slow it will go lumpy!)
- Spread the chocolate mixture on one of the cakes and place the other on top. Spread the remainder on the top and sides.
- The cake looks wonderful without any further decoration but if you like, you could sprinkle it with shavings of dark chocolate.

This is a cake to share and enjoy with friends.

If you have made this cake in advance and stored it in the fridge, make sure that you bring it to room temperature before eating (you could give it a quick whiz in the microwave.)

Rebecca Foggin 10

C hristmas pudding can vary enormously - I have never tasted a commercial one that can beat this recipe! It is moist, fruity and dark but with a light not solid texture. I really love making this recipe with children; there is lots of weighing, chopping, grating and stirring (which really needs to be done with Christmas carols in the background)!

The advantage of this recipe is that you can make it on Christmas Eve if you want to and it will still taste wonderful. I normally make it at the beginning of December and store it in the fridge.

Christmas pudding

50g SR flour
1 teaspoon nutmeg
1 teaspoon mixed spice
100g currants
100g raisins
100g sultanas
75g shredded vegetable suet
1 large tablespoon marmalade
100g soft brown sugar
75g fresh white breadcrumbs
1 cooking apple - grated
75g grated carrot
25g chopped peel
2 eggs
a wish

- Prepare all the ingredients.
- Put all the ingredients (except the last two) into a large bowl and mix.
- Lightly beat the eggs and add to the mixture.

- Mix very thoroughly and get everyone around you to have a stir and make a wish!
- Put the mixture into a pudding basin.
- Cover the top with greaseproof paper and cover with foil (make a pleat to allow for expansion).
- Tie string around the basin.
- Steam for 6 hours in a saucepan with a tightly fitting lid (water should be half way up the basin) or 3 - 4 hours in a pressure cooker - take care that it does not boil dry.

Store in a cool place or freeze until needed.
Steam for a further 3 hours on Christmas Day (or 1 - 2 hours in a pressure cooker).
It is not a good idea to microwave Christmas pudding due to it's very high sugar content.

Christmas puddings wrapped in calico make lovely presents, so make lots!

Lauren Rock 7

C hocolate chip cookies are sociable things to make and great for children to do. As they freeze well, you can do lots at a time and use them in packed lunches or as after school snacks.

Chocolate chip cookies

150 g soft margarine
200g caster sugar
2 eggs
300g SR flour (or 250g flour, 50g cocoa)
100g plain chocolate chips

- Put the margarine and sugar in a bowl and beat well until creamy.
- Add the eggs and beat well.
- Stir in the flour and chocolate chips and mix well until the flour is all combined (if the mixture is too stiff add a little water).
- Using a dessertspoon, place spoonfuls on the baking trays allowing room for the cookies to spread.
- Bake for 15 minutes 180 C Gas 4.
- Lift onto a cooling rack whilst still hot.

These cookies are also good for fund raising events as they are economical to make and always go like hot cakes!

Summer Rock 7

D ate and walnut cake is really moist, chewy and delicious - in theory it keeps very well, in practice I find it disappears very quickly!
This cake is relatively healthy being high in fibre and lower in fat than many other cakes.

Date and walnut cake

150ml hot water
250g dates - stoned and halved
150g margarine
125g soft brown sugar
2 tablespoons golden syrup
2 eggs
275g SR flour
50g walnuts - chopped

- Pour the hot water onto the dates and leave until cool.
- Put the margarine and sugar into the bowl and beat together until creamy.
- Add the syrup and eggs and beat well.
- Add the flour and then the dates as well as the soaking water, mix well.
- Stir in the walnuts.
- Put mixture into a lined 20 cm cake tin.
- Bake for approx. 1 hour 180 C Gas 4.

Try cooking mixture in two small loaf tins to create smaller slices.

D uck is quite a rich meat which is why I love to use it to make warm salads as it makes a more balanced dish. I love to add fresh peppery salad leaves, a good dressing and some lovely fresh bread.

Duck and shallot salad serves 4

2 large duck breasts
10 shallots - peeled and halved
20 cherry tomatoes
fresh rosemary sprigs
180g fine beans
6 cloves of garlic
6 tablespoons of olive oil
3 tablespoons white wine vinegar
mixed salad leaves
salt and pepper

- Place the duck breasts on a wire rack in a roasting dish and roast for 40 - 45 minutes 200 C Gas 6.
- Place the shallots in a separate baking dish and drizzle the olive oil over them, put in the oven at the same time as the duck and cook for 15 minutes, then add the rosemary, garlic and cherry tomatoes and return to the oven for a further 25 - 30 minutes.
- Put the fine beans in a pan of boiling water and cook for 10 minutes or until just cooked, then drain.
- Place the salad leaves in a big salad bowl, add the cooked beans.
- When the duck is cooked, remove from the oven, then slice and add to the salad.
- Remove the shallots and tomatoes and add to the salad, discard the rosemary.

- Squeeze the cooked garlic from their skins into the dish with the cooking juices from the tomatoes and olive oil, add salt and lots of freshly ground pepper and the wine vinegar, stir really well and pour onto the salad leaves, toss well to combine all the ingredients.
- Serve whilst still warm with some fresh bread.

If you go to France, look out for the tins of Duck confit as they are ideal for this dish if cooked well on a rack to remove the fat.

28

E aster biscuits are traditionally eaten during Easter week (which is from Palm Sunday to Easter Day). They should be quite large and are sometimes known as Easter cakes. It is worth making a large quantity as they make a lovely gift perhaps with some Spring flowers, as an alternative to chocolate.

Easter biscuits

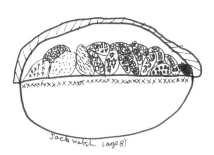

100g caster sugar
100g butter or margarine
1 egg beaten
200g plain flour
1 teaspoon mixed spice
50g currants

- Put the margarine and sugar in bowl and beat well until creamy.
- Add the egg and beat well.
- Add the flour, currants and spice, stir in with a tablespoon.
- Mix the mixture together until it makes a dough, then use your hands to make it into a ball, if it is too sticky add a little more flour.
- Chill for 30 minutes in the fridge.
- Roll out the dough carefully on a floured surface.
- Cut into 6 cm rounds and place on a baking tray.
- Bake for 10 - 15 minutes 180 C Gas 4.
- Lift off the tray whilst still warm and leave to cool on a wire rack.

The mixture may spread slightly when cooking so leave a little room between each one.

E aster nests must be the most simple thing to make. Toddlers and very young children love to stir in all the rice krispies and help to fill the paper cases - you will end up with chocolate everywhere but that is part of the fun!

Easter nests makes 24

150g milk or plain cooking chocolate
200g rice krispies
one bag of mini eggs

- Break up the chocolate into a bowl.
- Melt the chocolate by placing the bowl over a pan of boiling water and stir until melted, then remove from heat.
- Add the rice krispies and stir well until they are all coated in chocolate.
- Put large spoonfuls into some paper cases and make a dip in the middle.
- Whilst the chocolate is still soft, put some mini eggs on top.
- Leave to set.

Try using a different cereal. These are excellent fund raising cakes - easy, quick and children love them.

Kate Richards

10

30

F airy cakes are an essential part of growing up! Nothing is nicer than being in the kitchen with your Mum, Dad or Grandparent and helping to make a batch of cakes and then being allowed to decorate them as colourfully as you want! They are also the basis of many other cake and pudding recipes.

Fairy cakes

100g SR flour
100g soft margarine
100g caster sugar
2 eggs

100g icing sugar
2 tablespoons of water
decoration: smarties, sprinkles, cherries or coconut

12 paper cases

- Put the margarine and sugar into a bowl.
- Beat together well until light and creamy.
- Crack the eggs into a small bowl and beat lightly with a fork.
- Add the eggs and beat well to incorporate lots of air.
- Add the flour and fold in gently using a tablespoon until it is thoroughly mixed.
- Divide the mixture equally between 12 paper cases.
- Cook in a hot oven 200 C gas 6 for 15 minutes.
- Leave to cool.
- To make the icing, add the water to the icing sugar and beat well, then add the water carefully - if it is too runny add a little more icing sugar.

- Put a teaspoon of icing on each cake and decorate them colourfully.

Try adding cocoa powder to make chocolate cakes, lemon or orange rind, raisins or coconut. Alternatively, make butterfly cakes by filling the top with buttercream.

Leah m 8

Alice Telyer age 10

F ocaccia is an Italian flat bread flavoured with olive oil and rosemary and is delicious served with salads, soups and pasta. If you have a bread maker, double the recipe (except the yeast) and make two.

Focaccia

225g strong plain flour
half a teaspoon of salt
1 sachet of yeast
30ml olive oil
1 teaspoon sugar
sprigs of fresh rosemary
olive oil
sea salt

- Make the bread dough (see p 16).
- Grease and flour a baking tray.
- Roll out the dough to a 25 cm round.
- Place it on the baking tray.
- Leave to rise for 30 minutes until nice and puffy.
- Use your fingertips to make indents all over the dough.
- Drizzle over oil and put a rosemary sprig in each indent, sprinkle with sea salt.
- Bake 220 C Gas 7 for 20 minutes.

Replace the rosemary with olives, basil, tomatoes or onions.

Lucy Horn
Age 10

33

F ruit salad is a good opportunity to make the most of fruit which is in season. When there is not much available locally, make use of all the exotic fruits you can now buy. The important thing for a fruit salad is that it should have a range of colour and textures, to make it look attractive and taste exciting.

Fresh fruit salad

1 fresh pineapple
2 ripe pears
1 red skinned apple
1 mango
2 large oranges
a small bunch of black grapes
2 kiwi fruits
500ml fresh fruit juice eg apple, orange or pineapple

- Prepare the pineapple by cutting off the top and bottom and standing it on a chopping board remove the skin with a knife, then cut into slices, then smaller pieces, discarding the centre.
- Prepare the rest of the fruit and cut all the fruit to approximately the same size.
- Put all the fruit in a serving bowl and add enough fruit juice to cover the fruit.

Summer fruits and berries make a lovely dessert served with meringues.

G ingerbread biscuits can be made into many different shapes. You can cut the mixture into people, animals, letters, Christmas trees or stars as traditional decorations for the Christmas tree.

Gingerbread men

By Harry
Browning
Age 9

350g plain flour
125g margarine
1 teaspoon ground ginger or mixed spice
1 egg beaten
4 tablespoons of syrup
175g soft brown sugar
a few currants for eyes

- Put the margarine, sugar and syrup in a saucepan and heat gently until melted.
- Put the flour and ginger into a bowl and add the melted syrup mixture carefully with the egg.
- Mix everything together well and chill in a fridge for 1 hour.
- Flour the surface and roll out the mixture, cut out your shapes and place on a greased baking tray, add the eyes.
- Bake for 10 - 15 minutes 180 C Gas 4.
- Remove from the tray whilst still warm and leave to cool on a wire rack.

If you would like to ice the biscuits, do so at the last minute to avoid them going soft.

G oats cheese tarts are simple to make and can be eaten hot or cold. They can be made as big or small as you like and are great for picnics and parties.

Goats cheese tarts

1 packet of ready rolled puff pastry
6 ripe tomatoes
100g goats cheese
black olives
1 jar of pesto or to make your own see p 65

- Cut the pastry into eight equal pieces or to make bite size snacks use a pastry cutter to cut rounds.
- Place on a baking tray and spread with pesto.
- Slice the tomatoes thinly and arrange on top of the pesto.
- Either slice or crumble the goats cheese over the tomatoes and sprinkle the olives on top.
- Put in a hot oven Gas 7 220 C for 15 minutes.

These should be really full of flavour, so use vine ripened tomatoes if possible and home made pesto.

Thomas Smith
AGe 10

36

Hot cross buns are something I have always loved to make on Good Friday morning, the whole family can join in and the smell of the buns cooking is heavenly. They should be very sticky and are best eaten fresh. In medieval times the bakers marked the buns with a cross to ward off evil spirits.

Hot cross buns

450g strong plain flour
1 teaspoon salt
50g sugar
1 teaspoon mixed spice
100g dried fruit
50g margarine
250ml warm milk and water mixed
1 sachet of dried yeast

50g flour, 1 tablespoon oil and water for crosses
2 tablespoons sugar and 4 tablespoons water to glaze

- Put flour, salt, sugar, spice and margarine into bowl, rub in the margarine.
- Add dried fruit and yeast.
- Stir in the warm liquid and stir with a knife until the mixture forms a dough.
- Turn out onto the table and knead well for 5 minutes.
- Divide into 12 pieces and shape into buns, place on a baking tray.
- Leave to rise for one hour in a warm place until really spongy.
- Make the mixture for the crosses by mixing the flour, oil and enough water to make a smooth paste.

- Pipe crosses on top of the buns.
- Bake for 15 - 20 minutes 200 C Gas 6.
- Put the sugar and water into a saucepan and stir until dissolved.
- Brush over the cooked buns to glaze.

The dough should be quite sticky, then kneaded with more flour if necessary to give a really elastic mixture.

Callum Horn
10

H ummus is a garlicky dip made using a pestle and mortar and if you prefer a really smooth consistency use a food processor. It is great for picnics and packed lunches with lots of vegetable sticks and fresh pitta bread.

Hummus and pitta bread

1 can of chick peas
2 cloves of garlic - peeled
juice of half a lemon
olive oil
salt and pepper

- Put the garlic in the pestle and mortar and crush up to a paste adding salt and pepper and 1 teaspoon of oil.
- Add the chick peas and continue to blend together until smooth.
- Add the lemon juice and enough olive oil to make a good dipping consistency.
- Serve with sticks of red and green pepper, cucumber, celery and mini tomatoes.
- To make the pitta bread, use the bread recipe and roll each piece out to form an oval shape, don't leave to rise and cook in a hot oven for 10 minutes.

A hand blender is useful for this recipe.

I ce-cream is a lovely way to use fresh fruit in season. If you grow strawberries, raspberries, currants or plums or can visit a 'pick your own' then try making some.

Plum ice cream

450g dessert plums or damsons
100g caster sugar
50ml cold water
juice of half a lemon
425 ml double cream

- Cook the plums with the sugar and water, remove all the stones.
- Add the lemon juice and puree.
- Rub the puree through a sieve.
- Add more sugar if needed, chill for 30 minutes.
- Add the cream and stir well.
- Freeze in an ice-cream maker or pour into a plastic container and freeze, stirring at intervals to prevent large ice crystals forming.

You could replace some of the cream with a rich yoghurt.

Archie Wimborne Age: 8

40

J elly cups are a fun way to serve jelly and a variety of fruit shells could be used. It is better to set the jelly first then fill the shells just in case they leak.

Jelly cups

1 pack of orange jelly
500ml water
4 large oranges

- Prepare the oranges by cutting off the top third, then cut off a small amount from the base so that the orange doesn't wobble.
- Using a serrated knife, cut out the flesh from the orange, then cut the flesh up and put in a bowl with the juice, discarding the white pith.
- Make the jelly by placing the cubes in a measuring jug and add 280 ml boiling water, stir to dissolve.
- Add the orange pieces and juice and make up to 500 ml with cold water.
- Leave to set, then chop up.
- Fill the orange shells equally and replace the tops.

Don't use kiwi fruit in this recipe as the jelly won't set!

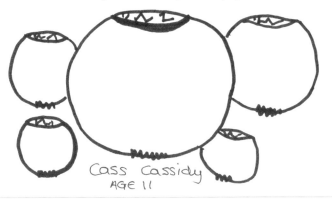

Cass Cassidy
AGE 11

41

K idneys are rich in iron and make a beautifully flavoured sauce to serve with pasta, rice or couscous.

Kidney ragu serves 4

6 lambs' kidneys
150g smoked streaky bacon - cut up
1 onion - diced
1 red pepper - sliced
2 cloves of garlic - chopped finely
2 tablespoons olive oil
mixed herbs, salt and pepper
1 glass of red wine
2 x 400g tins of chopped tomatoes

- Put the oil in a saucepan and gently sauté the onion, garlic and red pepper.
- Prepare the kidneys by cutting in half, remove the core with scissors and cut into quarters.
- Add the kidneys to the onion mixture with the bacon pieces and fry until the kidneys are coloured all over.
- Add the glass of red wine and allow to bubble and reduce for 5 minutes.
- Add the herbs, salt and pepper and tomatoes and simmer for 20 minutes.

This recipe is also good with liver cut into thin strips.

K ebabs are an easy way of cooking meat and vegetables all in one go. They can be prepared in advance and left to marinade. Experiment with different herbs and vegetables.

Kebabs makes 3 kebabs

1 chicken breast
1 tablespoon soy sauce
half an orange
1 clove of garlic
fresh or dried herbs eg basil, rosemary, thyme, oregano
2 tablespoons olive oil
6 mushrooms
1 red pepper
6 cherry tomatoes

- Cut the chicken into strips.
- Put the soy sauce, juice of half the orange, finely chopped garlic and olive oil into a bowl, add some fresh or dried herbs.
- Add the chicken to the marinade and leave to absorb the flavours.
- Cut the pepper into pieces and halve the mushrooms depending on their size.
- Put some foil to catch the drips and arrange the chicken and vegetables on the kebab sticks.
- Drizzle over the rest of the marinade and wrap in foil until needed.
- Cook under a hot grill for 10 minutes turning occasionally.

a kebab   by George Dennis

Honeyed vegetable kebabs

12 small new potatoes - cooked
2 courgettes - sliced thickly
1 red pepper - cut into squares
1 red onion - sliced and split into layers
6 button mushrooms

herb dressing
mint, coriander and basil - finely chopped
200ml crème fraiche

marinade
2 tablespoons olive oil
2 tablespoons honey
1 garlic clove
1 lemon
2 tablespoons wholegrain mustard
salt and freshly ground pepper

- Make the marinade and add the vegetables, leave to rest.
- Thread onto the skewers and cook for 10 minutes.
- Serve in toasted pitta breads with the herby dressing.

Soak wooden kebab sticks in water before using.

Kieran Ratcliffe   age 9

44

L amb curry is rich and beautifully flavoured. I like this combination of spices but adjust the amounts according to your taste. Try to buy small amounts of freshly ground spices or grind your own at home. If you prefer a hotter curry, add a little more chilli powder or use some fresh chilli peppers.

Lamb curry

0.5 kg lamb neck fillets
1 large onion, sliced
sunflower oil
2 cloves of garlic
2 teaspoons garam masala
2 teaspoons ground coriander
2 teaspoons ground cumin
1 teaspoon chilli powder
salt and pepper
150 g carton of passata
150 ml vegetable stock
200 ml coconut milk

- Trim some of the fat off the lamb and cut into cubes.
- Fry the onion until soft and lightly coloured, add the garlic and continue to cook.
- Add all the spices, stir over a medium heat for 2 - 3 minutes to cook.
- Add the lamb and stir in to the onion and spice mixture over a medium heat to colour the meat.
- Add the passata and stock and bring to the boil, turn down the heat and simmer for 1 hour.
- Add 200 ml coconut milk and continue to cook gently for 30 minutes.

- Taste the curry and adjust the seasoning, if there is too much sauce continue to cook until the sauce has reduced slightly.

I like to serve this with a vegetable curry, basmati rice and lots of side dishes such as mango chutney, cucumber, raita and naan bread.

Vegetable curry

So many different vegetables can be used to make a lovely curry. You could use new potatoes, fine beans, whole baby mushrooms, spinach, baby carrot, chick peas, aubergine, courgettes, sweet potato, cauliflower or green pepper. I use a mixture of four different vegetables using the new potatoes as a base.

Some of the vegetables will need pre-cooking and then add them to the same basic onion and spice mixture and toss well with a little stock and coconut milk. Serve very hot garnished with fresh coriander or mint leaves.

Johnathan Goves 3W   AGE 8

46

L emon meringue pie is my favourite pudding but it has to be home made to get the three layers perfect. It must have crisp pastry, a soft and very lemony filling and a light fluffy meringue which should be soft inside and very crispy on top. It is best served warm so that the texture and flavour of the filling is just right.

Lemon meringue pie

Pastry
200g flour
50g margarine
50g lard
100ml water

Filling
50g cornflour
300 ml water
2 large lemons, rind and juice
4 egg yolks
100g sugar

Eleanor Hurell

Meringue
4 egg whites
200g caster sugar

- Make the pastry following instructions p 64.
- Line a 30 cm flan tin, put some baking paper on the pastry and weigh down with pieces of excess pastry.
- Cook for 20 minutes 180 C Gas 4 removing paper for the last 5 minutes.
- Put the cornflour and a little of the water in a saucepan and blend together until smooth, add the remaining water and grated lemon rind and bring to the boil stirring continuously until thick.

47

- Remove from the heat and stir in the sugar, lemon juice and egg yolks.
- Return to a gentle heat and simmer for 3 minutes, stirring continuously to stop it catching on the bottom.
- Taste the mixture and add more sugar if needed, the consistency should be similar to custard, if it is too thin add one dessertspoon of cornflour mixed with a little water and pour into mixture, stirring over a gentle heat for 5 minutes.
- Pour the filling into the pastry case.
- To make the meringue, whisk the egg whites until stiff, add half the sugar and whisk again, then stir in the remainder.
- Spoon the meringue over the filling, covering it completely.
- Cook for 30 - 40 minutes 180 C Gas 4.

Use your own judgement to get the perfect filling as lemons vary. You may need more lemon or more sugar, just taste it and see.

Jamie Holliss

L emonade made with fresh lemons is refreshing and a perfect summer drink served with lots of ice. It is lovely for picnics and can also be made with oranges or mixed citrus fruits - adjust the sugar as needed.

Lemonade

2 - 3 lemons
4 - 6 tablespoons sugar
500ml water

- Wash the lemons.
- Peel the rind of the lemons with a potato peeler and place in a saucepan.
- Put 200 ml water in the saucepan and bring to the boil, simmer 5 minutes.
- Add the sugar and stir until dissolved.
- Leave to cool, add the rest of the water.
- Cut the lemons in half and juice the lemons.
- Add to the syrup mixture and stir.
- Strain the mixture and chill.
- Serve in tall glasses with ice and a sprig of mint.

Children love to help juice lemons, but potato peelers are tricky to use safely.

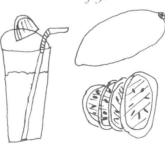

Sam Boren-Reast 6S age 11

Meatballs are fun for children to make and like beef burgers should be made using good quality meat and must be well seasoned. This recipe uses minced pork and is flavoured with apples and fresh thyme.

Pork and apple meatballs makes 20

500g lean minced pork
2 cooking apples
fresh thyme
2 cloves of garlic
salt and pepper

- Peel and grate the cooking apples and squeeze to remove the excess juice.
- Add the minced pork and finely chopped garlic, season well with freshly ground pepper and salt.
- Remove the leaves from the thyme stems and add to the mixture.
- Shape into balls.
- Put the meatballs in a roasting tin and cook for 30 minutes 200 C Gas 6.
- Serve with sweet pepper sauce as the peppers can be roasted at the same time.

Try lamb meatballs seasoned with mint or rosemary and serve with couscous.

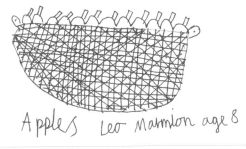

Apples   Leo Marmion age 8

50

Meringues are fantastic when they are light and crispy on the outside and slightly chewy in the middle but if you prefer them crispy all the way through, just cook them longer (if you want to keep them they will need to be dried completely).

Meringues

2 egg whites
100g caster sugar

- Separate the eggs carefully and put the egg whites in a clean dry bowl.
- Whisk the egg whites until stiff.
- Add half the sugar and whisk again, then fold in the remaining sugar.
- Line a baking tray with baking paper.
- Either pipe the meringue mixture onto the tray or use a tablespoon to drop spoonfuls of the mixture onto tray.
- Cook in a very low oven 150 C Gas for 1½ hours, or slightly longer for meringues you want to keep.
- Store in an airtight container.

To make a really good meringue, it is vital that the bowl and whisk are grease free and that there isn't a trace of egg yolk in the mixture.

M ince pie making is definitely one of my favourite ways to spend a December afternoon. I always make lots because they are lovely things to share and always seem to disappear very quickly! Children love to help roll out the pastry and fill the pies.

Mince pies makes approx. 28

400g flour
100g hard margarine
100g lard
water to mix
1 large jar of mincemeat

- Put flour, marg and lard into a bowl, use your fingertips to rub in until the mixture looks like breadcrumbs.
- Add enough water to make a dough.
- Roll out half the dough and cut out 24 circles to line two bun trays.
- Put a teaspoonful of mincemeat into each pastry base and use some water to dampen around the edges lightly.
- Roll out 24 tops using a slightly smaller cutter and place on top of the mincemeat.
- Press the edges together to seal and cook for 20 minutes 200 C Gas 6.

Seal the pies well and don't overfill them.

Muesli bars were created due to excess muesli in the cupboard which wasn't being eaten. They make a really delicious mid morning nibble and are great for lunch boxes and after school snacks.

Muesli bars

4 tablespoons golden syrup or honey
200g margarine
100g brown sugar
300g muesli
200g SR flour

- Put the golden syrup, margarine and brown sugar in a saucepan and heat gently until the margarine is melted. (Alternatively, put in a mixing bowl and pop in the microwave.)
- Stir in the muesli and flour and stir thoroughly until combined.
- Press into a swiss roll tin and cook for 30 minutes 180 C Gas 4.
- Cut into squares and lift onto a cooling rack.

Any type of muesli can be used to make these or use porridge oats and add some dried fruit and nuts.

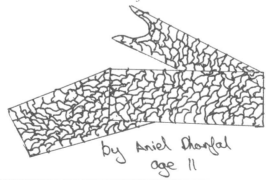

by Aniel Dhanjlal
age 11

M uffins are traditionally a crumpet-like mixture but the American muffin is more cake-like and is traditionally flavoured with blueberries, banana or chocolate chip, all of which are delicious, but also try adding raspberries, blackcurrants or apple.

Raspberry muffins

2 eggs
100 ml milk
75g margarine - softened
150g SR flour
100g caster sugar
1 teaspoon baking powder
100g frozen raspberries

- Whisk the egg and milk together.
- Beat the softened margarine with the sugar, add the egg and milk, flour, baking powder and mix well.
- Stir in the raspberries carefully.
- Divide between 10 muffin cases.
- Bake for 20 minutes Gas 6 200 C.
- Eat whilst still warm.

To make double chocolate chip muffins, instead of the raspberries, substitute 100g chocolate chips and 25g cocoa powder.

54

N ew potatoes are such a special flavour and texture and this salad really makes the most of them. This is lovely served with herby cooked chicken or grilled fish.

New potato salad serves 4 - 6

750g small new potatoes
8 tablespoons extra virgin olive oil
3 tablespoons white wine vinegar
fresh mint
2 cloves of garlic - finely chopped
1 bunch of spring onions
1 bunch of watercress
salt and freshly ground black pepper

- Scrub the new potatoes and boil for approximately 20 minutes or until soft.
- In a serving bowl put the extra virgin olive oil, wine vinegar, salt and pepper and finely chopped mint and garlic.
- Whisk well together to combine, then add the finely sliced spring onion.
- When the potatoes are cooked, drain them well and stir them into the dressing whilst hot so that they absorb all the lovely flavours.
- Wash and trim the watercress and toss through the potatoes.

This recipe is lovely for Summer lunches and picnics.

N utty date squares are deliciously chewy, and with the dates, walnuts and oats are high in fibre and are perfect with a mid morning cup of tea or coffee.

Nutty date squares makes 12

175g flour, wholemeal, plain or SR
175g oats
200g margarine
100g brown sugar

Filling
250g stoned dates - chopped
50g walnuts
2 tablespoons water
1 tablespoon clear honey

- Place filling ingredients in a pan and simmer until dates are soft.
- Mix flour and oats together, stir in sugar.
- Rub in fat.
- Place half the mixture in a lined tin approx. 25 cm x 20 cm and press down.
- Cover with the date mixture.
- Sprinkle over the remaining oat mixture and press down to cover the dates.
- Bake 180 C Gas 4 35 - 40 minutes.
- Leave to cool in the tin then cut into 12 slices.

Use your fingers to spread and flatten the mixture - it's the easiest way.

Oaties remind me of family holidays as Mum always made them for long car journeys and camping trips. I make them regularly for snacks and packed lunches because they are very quick and easy to make, keep well and everyone loves them.

Chocolate oaties

200g margarine
100g caster sugar
200g SR flour
200g rolled oats
50g cocoa powder
2 tablespoons golden syrup
200g icing sugar
25g cocoa powder
50ml water

- Melt the margarine gently in a saucepan with the syrup, sugar and cocoa.
- Add the flour and oats and stir well to combine all the ingredients.
- Press into a baking tin approx. 20 x 30 cm.
- Cook 180 C Gas 4 for 30 minutes.
- Leave to cool in tin.
- Make the icing by combining the icing sugar, cocoa and water.
- Spread over the oaties and leave to set before cutting into 16 slices.

Try muesli instead of some of the oats.

O range pork came about because I wanted to make a simple sauce for some pork steaks. I didn't have any apple juice so I thought I would give orange juice a try and my family loved it! It is delicious served with creamy mashed potatoes and a really fresh savoy cabbage.

Orange pork

4 pork loin steaks
1 large onion
2 cloves of garlic
sunflower oil
salt and freshly ground black pepper
1 large teaspoon of dried mixed herbs
300ml orange juice

- Slice the onion thinly and sauté gently in olive oil, add the crushed garlic.
- Season the pork well with the freshly ground salt and black pepper and add to the sauté pan.
- Cook the meat for 5 minutes on each side to seal and brown the meat.
- Sprinkle with the dried herbs, add the orange juice and bring to the boil.
- Turn down the heat, cover the pan with a lid and simmer for 40 minutes, or transfer the mixture to a casserole and continue to cook in the oven.

I normally trim the fat off the pork for this dish.

O range pudding is really light and fluffy and is easy to make, particularly if you have a little cake to use up. It should be very zesty so it is good to make when oranges are at their best in January.

Orange pudding

2 large oranges
50g caster sugar
50g cake crumbs
150ml milk
2 eggs - separated
25g margarine

- Put the margarine, sugar and the zest of both oranges in a bowl, beat together.
- Add the cake crumbs.
- Warm the milk and pour over the crumb mixture.
- Juice the oranges, and add to the mixture with the two egg yolks, beat together.
- Whisk the egg whites until they are stiff and carefully fold into the mixture.
- Spoon into a 20 cm dish.
- Cook for 30 minutes 180 C Gas 4.

This is also good in small ramekins; if you want a more citrus flavour add the zest of a lemon. Kumquats make a lovely accompaniment to this dessert.

P ain au raisin conjures up images of hot Summers and canoeing on the Dordogne. I tried to re-create them as part of a French cooking morning at school with thirty eight year olds. We had great fun and the results, whilst not completely authentic, were delicious, particularly when eaten still warm.

Pain au raisin

1 packet of ready rolled puff pastry
1 pot of fresh vanilla custard
150g raisins

- Lay out the puff pastry and spread with about four tablespoons of the fresh custard.
- Sprinkle the raisins over the custard.
- Roll up the pastry from the long side and seal the edge with water.
- Cut the roll into slices 1 - 2 cm thick and place them on a baking tray.
- Cook in a hot oven 200 C for 10 minutes.

These are very quick and easy to make, these will be quite small pain au raisin, to make bigger ones roll up from the short end.
I think that French pain au raisin uses a yeast based dough, which also works well. Use a sweet dough and roll it out thinly to a square.

by Nathan Jayne age 10

60

P ancakes are traditionally eaten on Shrove Tuesday as people used to eat up foods which were forbidden in Lent. Across the world, Mardi Gras celebrations and carnivals are enjoyed and in many parts of Britain (including Chandlings) pancake races are held.

Pancakes

200g plain flour
500 ml milk (or soya milk)
2 large eggs
oil
To serve: lemon and sugar

- Place the flour in a mixing bowl and make a well in the centre.
- Add the eggs and 250 ml of the milk.
- Mix with a wooden spoon until it forms a smooth paste with no lumps.
- Add the rest of the milk gradually, stirring hard all the time.
- Pour the batter into a measuring jug.
- Pour a little oil into a frying pan and heat.
- Pour a thin layer of the batter evenly over the base of the pan and cook for 1 - 2 minutes, when all the 'wet bits' are set then turn over and cook on the other side.
- Serve straight away, rolled or folded with lots of lemon and sugar.

They say that 'the first pancake is always a lump' so don't worry if your first try sticks, it is probably because the pan isn't quite the right temperature.

P arkin is such an old fashioned cake but I love this recipe and it is perfect with a big cup of tea after a walk. The one problem is that it really is so much better if you leave it at least three days before you eat it and that takes a lot of willpower!

Parkin

250g SR flour or SR wholemeal
250g rolled oats
125g margarine
125g black treacle
125g golden syrup
125g soft brown sugar
170ml milk

- Place the margarine, treacle, syrup and sugar in a saucepan and heat gently until the fat has melted, remove from heat.
- Put the flour and oats in a bowl and add the melted ingredients and also the milk.
- Mix all the ingredients thoroughly.
- Line a 20 cm cake tin with baking paper and pour in the mixture.
- Bake in a medium hot oven 180 C Gas 4 for approximately 1 hour until the cake feels firm to touch.
- Leave to cool for 10 minutes before turning out onto a cooling rack.
- When cold, put the cake in an airtight container and leave for three days before eating.

Adjust the cooking time according to the size and shape of the tin you are using.

P asta is such a versatile food, children love it and it is possible to cook a meal with a simple sauce very quickly and easily. You can buy a fantastic range of dried and fresh pasta now but making your own is very satisfying and a fun activity to do with children of all ages.

Pasta

200g strong plain flour
2 large fresh free range eggs
semolina flour for dusting

- Put the flour in a bowl and make a well in the centre, add the eggs and using a fork, bring the mixture together to form a dough.
- Use your hands and knead well for 10 minutes until it is very smooth and elastic.
- Wrap it in cling film and leave to rest for at least 30 minutes in the fridge.
- Flour the work surface and your hands with the semolina flour and roll out the dough, rolling then turning, adding more flour if needed until it is very thin.
- Sprinkle with a little more flour and roll up the dough like a swiss roll.
- Cut the roll into slices about 2 cm wide.
- Put the tagliatelle in a large pan of fast boiling water and cook for 3 minutes.
- Drain well and mix with a simple sauce such as the pesto or sweet pepper sauce.

To make a better tagliatelle use a pasta machine which rolls and cuts the dough evenly.

P astry making needs practice, but it is worth persevering with as it is so much better than the commercial alternatives (except puff pastry which is better to buy). Shortcrust pastry should be very light, crisp and crumbly and to achieve this, handle it as little as possible and with cool, gentle hands.

Shortcrust pastry

200g flour
50g hard margarine
50g lard or white vegetable fat
100ml cold water

- Put the flour, margarine and lard into a bowl, using your fingertips rub the fat into the flour until it looks crumbly (it is important not to over rub it to avoid the mixture getting warm and sticky).
- Add the water gradually, stirring with a knife until the mixture forms a dough which leaves the sides of the bowl.
- Put it onto a lightly floured surface and roll out to the shape desired by rolling and turning, using more flour if needed.

The secret of good pastry is really in the light handling, but the quality of the flour is also important. It is traditional to use plain flour but I have always used self raising with good results.

George 4R Ruck age 9

P esto is a famous Italian sauce which can be stirred into pasta, added to soups or used as a base for the goats cheese tarts on p 36.
Making pesto is an amazing sensory experience, the smell of the basil, garlic, toasted pine nuts and parmesan cheese are incredible and making it in a pestle and mortar means that you feel and see the ingredients being combined.
Alternatively, a food processor will do the job much quicker!

Pesto

50g fresh basil leaves
10g coarse sea salt
25g pine nuts
2 cloves of garlic
50g fresh parmesan, grated
125ml olive oil

- Toast the pine nuts by putting them in a dry saucepan over a medium heat and shake them to prevent burning.
- Put the pine nuts, garlic, salt and basil into a pestle and mortar, grind together.
- Add a little of the cheese and continue to grind.
- Add the rest of the cheese a little at a time, then gradually add the oil, grinding and mixing until it is all incorporated.

Use extra virgin olive oil for the best flavour.
If you prefer a smoother sauce, use a hand blender or food processor.

P udsey bear supports the 'Children in Need' appeal which raises an amazing amount of money each year for children in the U.K. who need help. Cake sales are always an excellent way to raise money and children can be involved in the organisation, baking and selling of the cakes and biscuits. Lakeland sell Pudsey bear cake cases, biscuit cutters and bags through their mail order catalogue and support the charity.

Pudsey bear biscuits makes 12 large bears

PUDSEY BEAR

100g hard margarine
100g caster sugar
1 egg
275g flour

- Put flour, margarine and sugar in a mixing bowl, rub in using your fingertips.
- Add the egg and mix with a knife to form a dough, add a little more flour if it is too soft, or a drop of water if it is too crumbly.
- Chill in the fridge for 30 minutes.
- Roll out the dough on a floured surface and cut out using your Pudsey bear cutter.
- Place carefully on a baking tray and cook for 10 minutes 180 C Gas 4.
- Lift off the baking tray and cool on a rack.
- Use ready to roll icing to make Pudsey's spotty headband.

Make lots of biscuits, help organise a cake sale and send lots of money to Children in Need. If you would like to know what your donation could provide see www.bbc.co.uk/pudsey

Queen cakes are a very traditional recipe. They are good to make if you have some pastry left from making a pie and can be varied depending on the type of jam used, but I think they are best with home made raspberry jam. Like most cakes, they freeze well and so it's worth making a lot at a time.

Queen cakes makes 24

200g flour
50g margarine
50g lard
raspberry jam
100g SR flour
100g caster sugar
2 eggs
zest of 1 lemon
100g margarine

- Make the pastry (see p 64).
- Use a 7 cm pastry cutter to cut out 24 rounds and use to line 2 x 12 hole bun tins.
- Place a teaspoonful of jam at the bottom of each pastry case.
- Cream the margarine and sugar together, then beat in the eggs thoroughly.
- Stir in the lemon zest and flour.
- Place a spoonful of the mixture on top of the jam and spread carefully to cover.
- Cook for 15 - 20 minutes 200 C Gas 6.
- Cool on a cooling rack.

The zest of the lemon is just the lemon coloured peel on the outside and contains lots of flavour.

R ed cabbage and apple is so delicious and is worth making a big oven full and then freezing it to serve with chicken, pork, sausages and of course the Christmas turkey.

If you have a food processor it makes the slicing of the onions and cabbage so much easier.

Red cabbage and apple

900g red cabbage (1 small cabbage)
450g onions
450g apples (cox or cooking)
4 tablespoons of wine vinegar
3 tablespoons brown sugar
2 garlic cloves - crushed
salt and pepper
250ml stock, red wine or water

- Cut the red cabbage in half and remove the core, slice thinly.
- Peel and slice the onions.
- Peel and chop the apples.
- Put these ingredients into a large casserole dish with plenty of salt and pepper, the garlic and brown sugar.
- Pour the stock and wine vinegar over the vegetables.
- Cover the casserole with a lid or foil and cook slowly for 2 hours Gas 4 180 C adding more liquid if necessary.

Freeze the red cabbage in small quantities and then reheat in the microwave, try adding a little cinnamon to the mixture to add to the flavour.

R oasted vegetables are a wonderfully easy way to cook vegetables and the type can be varied according to what is in season, try squash, parsnips, asparagus, baby carrots or beetroot. Use plenty of fresh herbs and good olive oil. These vegetables can be served in a pastry case with a nice crisp salad as a light meal or as an accompaniment to chicken, sausages or lamb.

Roasted vegetables and couscous

300g couscous
700ml boiling water
red onion, peeled and cut into quarters
6 cloves of garlic
vine ripened tomatoes - halved
aubergines - cut into chunks
red, yellow and orange peppers
mushrooms
sweet potatoes
courgettes cut into chunks
fresh basil, rosemary or thyme
salt and pepper
olive oil

- Peel and cut the sweet potatoes into chunks, boil for 10 minutes, then drain.
- Prepare all the vegetables and cut into large chunks, approximately the same size.
- Put the vegetables and sweet potatoes in a large roasting tin and sprinkle with olive oil and plenty of salt and pepper, toss the vegetables in the oil.
- Add the garlic and torn basil leaves (or other herbs) to the vegetables.
- Put in a hot oven 200 C Gas 6 for 30 minutes.

- Put the couscous in a saucepan with a lid and pour over the boiling water, leave for 10 minutes for the couscous to absorb the water and fluff up with a fork.
- When the vegetables are cooked, remove to a hot serving dish and stir the remaining oil into the couscous, check for seasoning, adding more salt, pepper and chopped herbs if needed.

You may need two trays as the vegetables roast better if they are not too crowded.
Roast lamb studded with garlic and rosemary, herby couscous and roasted vegetables is one of my family's favourite meals and is easier to prepare than a traditional roast dinner.

Katie Beasley age 8

R hubarb is a really British fruit and makes the best ever crumble but also makes a good 'fool' when mixed with custard and cream. I am lucky enough to have a good supply of rhubarb from my Mum and Dad's garden. If you don't know someone who grows it, try farmers markets and farm shops for really freshly picked stems in Spring.

Rhubarb fool

350 ml sweetened cooked rhubarb
25g caster sugar
25g custard powder
175ml milk
125ml whipping cream

- Prepare the custard by blending 50 ml milk with the custard powder and sugar. Heat the remaining milk and pour over the paste. Return to the pan and bring to the boil, stirring all the time.
- Leave to cool.
- Whip the cream until just peaked (take care not to overwhip).
- Mix the rhubarb and custard together, then carefully fold in the cream. Taste and add more sugar if needed.
- Chill and serve with shortbread or meringues.

Rhubarb is very high in calcium. Either use the forced rhubarb available in January or wait for the first of the outdoor rhubarb in April. Both are so delicious and very easy to grow in your garden.

S almon, cooked all on one tray with lots of herbs and vegetables, makes the perfect quick supper dish. It is full of flavour, very healthy and looks really appealing.

Herby baked salmon

4 salmon fillets
20 small cherry tomatoes
1 lemon - cut into quarters
500g small new potatoes - scrubbed
200g fine beans
1 handful of fresh basil
extra virgin olive oil
salt and pepper
2 sweet pointed orange peppers
2 cloves of garlic

- Boil the potatoes and beans until just cooked then drain.
- Cut the pepper into quarters lengthwise and remove the seeds.
- Put the salmon fillets, tomatoes, lemon and pepper into a large roasting tin.
- Add the drained potatoes and beans.
- Add some olive oil, salt and pepper, torn basil leaves and garlic, and use your hands to coat all the ingredients.
- Roast in a hot oven 220 C Gas 7 for 15 minutes, and serve immediately.

This is delicious served with olive or tomato bread.

S cones remind me of Sunday tea, Summer picnics and lovely home made raspberry jam. Home made scones are so much better than anything you can buy and they really do take 30 minutes to make and cook from start to finish. I have always found that the quicker I make them, the better they are!

Scones

400g SR flour
100g hard margarine or butter
50g sugar
100g sultanas (optional)
300ml milk

- Put flour, sugar and margarine in a bowl.
- Rub the margarine into the flour with your fingertips.
- Stir in the sultanas.
- Add most of the milk and stir with a knife to form a soft dough, add more milk if necessary a little at a time.
- Put the dough on a floured surface and roll or pat out until it is no thinner than 2 cm (I use the blade of a knife as a guide).
- Cut out rounds with a pastry cutter and re-roll gently any trimmings.
- Place the scones on a baking tray and place in a pre-heated oven 220 C Gas 7 for 10 - 15 minutes depending on size of scone.
- When cooked transfer to a cooling rack.

For the best scones, handle the dough as little as possible, have cool hands and eat whilst still warm.

S hortbread can be tricky to make as the dough is often too crumbly but this recipe is foolproof and perfect every time as it uses a melting method. Shortbread is a wonderful accompaniment to fresh raspberries or strawberries in Summer.

Shortbread

200g butter or hard margarine
200g plain flour
100g cornflour
100g caster sugar

- Put the butter or margarine into a saucepan.
- Warm gently until it is just melted.
- Put the flour, cornflour and caster sugar into a mixing bowl.
- Add the melted butter and stir well.
- Press the mixture into a 20 cm round baking tin, decorate the edges with a fork.
- Cook 180 C Gas 4 for 30 - 40 minutes.
- Mark into slices whilst warm but leave to cool before lifting from the tin.

The addition of the cornflour gives the shortbread its 'short' texture, a bit messy to eat but delicious.

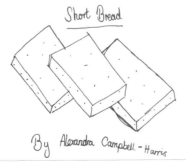

Short Bread

By Alexandra Campbell - Harris

S ausage and bean casserole is just right for a cold winters day. It takes a while to cook so I always double the recipe so that I can put some in the freezer for another day. Serve with jacket potatoes and a green vegetable for a nutritious, filling and economical family meal.

Sausage and bean casserole serves 4 - 6

1 large onion - sliced
2 cloves of garlic - finely sliced
a little oil
6 pork and apple sausages
1 kg diced pork
2 apples eg Coxes - sliced
400g tin haricot or black eyed beans
500g carton passata
2 x 400g tins chopped tomatoes
250 ml apple juice
fresh or dried basil or thyme
salt and freshly ground pepper

- Put the sliced onion and garlic in a large saucepan, sauté until soft.
- Cut each sausage into three and add to pan, stir over a medium heat for 2 - 3 minutes.
- Add the diced pork and stir on a medium heat until coloured on all sides.
- Put the meat and onion mixture in a large casserole, add the apple slices.
- Put the beans, passata, tinned tomatoes, apple juice and seasonings into the pan and bring to the boil.
- Pour the sauce over the meat mixture and mix well to combine all the ingredients.

75

- Cover the casserole with either a lid or foil and place in a medium oven Gas 4 180 C for 2 - 3 hours.

Children love to help make this dish and can chop up the sausages and apple and help stir all the ingredients together in the casserole.

S pring rolls can be made as big or as small as you like and make perfect little bites to serve at parties and buffets. You can vary the ingredients as they are also lovely with cooked chicken or duck. If I am serving them as a main course, I make them into parcels rather than rolls and serve them with a spicy tomato sauce and rice.

Spring rolls

1 packet of filo pastry
1 red pepper
100g mushrooms
1 bunch of spring onions
1 clove of garlic
1 packet of beansprouts
200g prawns, defrosted
hoi sin sauce
vegetable oil

- Cut the red pepper, mushrooms and spring onions into strips and crush the garlic.
- Put a little oil in a sauté pan and add the pepper, mushrooms, spring onions and garlic, cook gently until softened then add the beansprouts and prawns and continue to cook for 3 - 4 minutes, leave to cool slightly.
- Separate the filo leaves and place two layers together on your worksurface, spread a thin layer of hoi sin sauce onto the pastry, then place a spoonful of the stir fry mixture on one end.
- Dampen down the edges of the pastry with water then fold the long edges over to enclose the filling, damp the edges again and roll up carefully.

- Make sure that the rolls are sealed thoroughly, then transfer to an oiled baking tray.
- Continue making the rolls until you have used up all your filling.
- Cook in a hot oven for 20 minutes.
- Eat immediately when cooked with a spicy tomato sauce and rice.

You need to work quickly when making the rolls or the pastry can become soggy and fall apart when you transfer them to a baking tray.

To make tiny ones suitable to serve with drinks, use half a sheet of filo and fold in quarter. Spread with a little mango chutney and place some cooked duck (duck confit is ideal) and a little spring onion.

Wet the edges with water, fold the sides in first, then roll up, sealing the end securely. Cook for 10 minutes and serve hot.

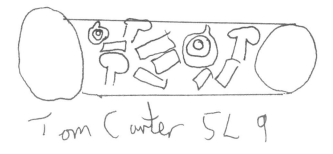

S wiss rolls are really good fun to make and are not difficult as long as you weigh ingredients accurately and follow the instructions very carefully. Children really enjoy rolling them up with lots of jam inside. Swiss rolls are fatless sponges and because of this they don't keep well and should be eaten within two days.

Swiss roll

4 eggs
100g caster sugar and a little extra to sprinkle
100g SR flour
raspberry jam

- Take a really clean bowl and crack 4 eggs into it, add the caster sugar.
- Using an electric hand mixer, whisk the mixture until it is thick and creamy. (To tell whether it is thick enough, lift the whisk out of the mixture and 'draw' your initial, does the letter stay for about 8 seconds on the surface? if not, whisk a little longer.)
- Sieve the flour into the mixture and fold it in gently, using a metal spoon - Check that there are no pockets of flour left, but take care not to over mix it or you will lose the air.
- Line a 24 cm x 35 cm baking tray with baking paper and pour the mixture in, tilt the tray to make sure the mixture is in all corners.
- Cook in a hot oven 220 C Gas 8 for 12 minutes.
- Put some more baking paper onto the work surface and sprinkle with caster sugar.
- Take the swiss roll from the oven and quickly turn it onto the sugared paper.

- Remove the paper from the swiss roll and spread with jam, make sure you go right to the edges but take care not to dig into the sponge. *You must work quickly because if the sponge cools it will crack when you try to roll it up.*
- Use the paper under the sponge to help you roll the swiss roll, fold over the short edge of the sponge nearest you, then hold the paper and use it to roll the swiss roll away from you.
- Leave to cool with the join underneath.
- To make a chocolate swiss roll, replace 25g of the flour with cocoa powder and when you take it out of the oven, roll it up with baking paper inside until it is cool, then unroll it and spread with chocolate butter icing, then roll up again.

Remember: whisk the mixture until it is very thick and creamy, fold in the flour very gently, don't over cook it (sponge should just spring back when you touch it) and work as quickly as possible when spreading the jam and rolling up……. Easy!

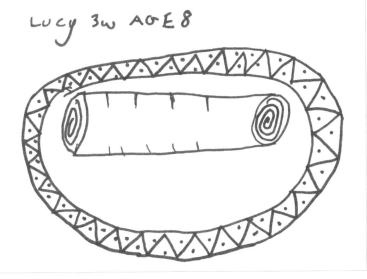

80

S moothies are ideal breakfast foods. They give a good vitamin boost and can be made with various combinations of fruits such as oranges, grapefruits, peaches, plums, apricots or other seasonal soft fruits. Smoothies can be made with or without milk or yoghurt but for children whole milk will provide extra energy, calcium, and vitamins.

Mango and raspberry smoothie

1 mango, peeled and stoned
1 banana
75g raspberries
100ml milk

Mango, peach and orange smoothie

1 ripe mango, peeled and stoned
juice of 1 large orange
1 ripe peach, peeled and stoned

Banana and pineapple smoothie

3 bananas
half a fresh pineapple, skinned and core removed
3 tablespoons of natural yoghurt

- Puree all the ingredients together in a liquidiser and drink immediately.

Smoothies can also be made using a spoonful of cooked fruit eg mixed summer berries, add a little sugar or honey if needed.

81

S ummer pudding is special to make and to eat because it really epitomises an English Summer day. The best way to buy the fruit is to go to a 'Pick your own' or Farmers market because the fruit should be very fresh. The choice of fruit can vary but I normally include strawberries, raspberries, redcurrants and blackcurrants.

Summer pudding

750g mixed soft fruits
100g caster sugar
2 tablespoons of water
4 - 5 slices of white bread

- Prepare the fruit, wash gently and remove stalks and leaves, cut the strawberries in half.
- Put the fruit in a saucepan with the water and sugar, simmer gently until the fruit is softened and juicy.
- Line a pudding basin with bread, cutting it to fit round the bowl but about 3 cm higher than the edge.
- Fill the lined bread with the fruit and juices.
- Fold the top of the bread down and place another piece of bread on top.
- Place a saucer on top of the pudding and weigh it down with something heavy.
- Chill overnight in the fridge.
- Serve with lots of cream.

If you have any juices left, either serve with the pudding, or freeze to use as a coulis with another dessert.

Tea bread is a fatless cake, which is great for snacks, lunch boxes and with a cup of tea in the afternoon, perhaps sliced with butter.
It is high in fibre because of the dried fruit but this could be further increased by using wholemeal self raising flour.

Teabread

120g currants
120g sultanas
120g raisins
150g brown sugar
zest of 1 lemon and 1 orange
250g SR flour
1 large egg
250ml tea

- Put dried fruit and sugar in a bowl and pour over the hot tea.
- Leave the fruit to soak for 3 hours or overnight.
- Beat in the egg, orange and lemon zest and flour.
- Line a 1 kg loaf tin with baking paper and pour the mixture into it.
- Cook for 1 hour 30 minutes Gas 4 180 C.

A thin slice of this cake will provide an energising and satisfying snack. Try to use good quality dried fruit and experiment with other fruits like apricots, figs and dried peaches or even a few nuts.

T omato soup is a wonderful way to use that sudden glut of tomatoes in late Summer. If you can use home grown ones that are really ripe and juicy, then the flavour will be superb and they are so easy to grow in a small space.

Tomato and basil soup

1 onion, finely chopped
2 tablespoons of oil
1 large clove of garlic
1 kg ripe tomatoes, chopped
750ml stock
2 tablespoons tomato puree
4 tablespoons torn basil leaves
black pepper and sea salt
150ml double cream (optional)

- Fry the onion and garlic gently.
- Stir in the tomatoes, puree and stock.
- Bring to the boil and simmer for 30 minutes.
- Whizz in a food processor and then sieve to remove the pips.
- Return to the heat and add the torn basil leaves and plenty of salt and pepper.
- Reheat gently and stir in the cream if used.
- Serve with torn basil leaves and plenty of fresh bread.

This recipe is also good with the addition of red peppers, which I normally roast first until soft.

agliatelle with baby vegetables is a really fresh and lovely light meal, and so easy to make. I like it with smoked salmon, but a vegetarian version would be just as good. This works with so many different vegetables that every time I make it, it is slightly different, depending on the season and availability. If you grow your own vegetables and can pick baby beetroot, carrots, courgettes, beans, peas or tomatoes then this recipe is perfect.

Tagliatelle with baby vegetables

dried tagliatelle
2 cloves of garlic
1 red pepper, sliced into strips
1 orange pepper, sliced into strips
10 cherry tomatoes
mangetout
baby corn
baby courgettes, chunks
200g smoked salmon
vegetable oil
fresh herbs eg basil, tarragon or rosemary
150ml single cream
salt and pepper
1 lemon and parsley

- Fill a large pan with water and bring to the boil.
- Prepare all the vegetables, heat a large sauté pan or wok with a little oil and sauté the baby corn, courgettes, peppers, garlic and cherry tomatoes. Add salt and pepper and the fresh herbs.

- Add the tagliatelle to the water whilst you sauté the vegetables and boil rapidly for the time indicated on the packet.
- When the tagliatelle is almost cooked, stir in the cream to the vegetables and lastly stir in the smoked salmon.
- Drain the tagliatelle and put into a warmed serving dish. Add the salmon and vegetable mixture and sprinkle over some finely chopped parsley and a squeeze of lemon juice.
- Serve with a slice of lemon and some fresh tomato or olive bread.

It is difficult to give quantities for this because it depends on which vegetables you choose to use, and because it can be adapted so easily to serve 2 or 12. If you have problems sautéing all the vegetables in a pan, roast them in the oven instead (you may need to slightly pre-cook some of the root vegetables) and just add the cream and salmon to the roasting tin at the end.

James Hand 6C age 10

Tartes aux fruits are so satisfying to make because they look wonderful but are really very easy to put together. We made these with pain au raisin in a French cooking morning at school. The children enjoyed being creative arranging all the fresh fruit and loved eating them!

Tartes aux pommes

1 packet of ready rolled puff pastry
4 red skinned apples, cut into quarters and core removed
apricot jam or honey

- Lay the puff pastry out and cut into eight rectangles.
- Slice the apples thinly and lay on the pastry, overlapping each slice slightly.
- Cook for 15 minutes at 200 C Gas 6.
- Warm four tablespoons of apricot jam or honey and brush over the apples.
- Return to the oven for 5 minutes.
- Eat whilst still warm.

This very simple recipe works just as well with pears, and also looks good as a large tart. Cut out a large circle of puff pastry and arrange the apples or pears in circles.

Abigail McGill
age 9.

87

Tartes aux fruits

200g shortcrust pastry
fresh vanilla custard
4 different fresh fruits eg strawberries, raspberries, grapes, kiwi, peach,
mango, blackberries, pears, red skinned apples
apricot jam or redcurrent jelly

- Use the pastry to line eight individual tartlet tins (or shallow Yorkshire pudding trays are good).
- Scrunch up some baking paper and put in the bottom of each to help them keep their shape.
- Cook for 10 minutes at 180 C Gas 4 then remove the paper and cook for a further 5 minutes.
- Leave to cool.
- Put a tablespoon of custard in the bottom of each tart.
- Prepare the fruit and arrange a selection on top of each tart.
- Warm the redcurrent jelly or apricot jam and use to brush over the fruit carefully.

Use a good quality fresh vanilla custard and, if you like. stir in some crème fraiche before spooning into the pastry case. The pastry will go soggy after a while, so eat within a couple of hours of making if possible.

Thomas Browne 9

88

Tetbury is a lovely Cotswold town with a beautiful hotel on the outskirts called Calcot Manor. In May 2004 the hotel ran a competition to find a recipe for a Tetbury tart. The brief was to design a recipe that reflected the produce of Gloucestershire and use some of the 'Duchy Organics' products. I spent a long time devising a recipe and was lucky to have family and friends willing to try so many different variations over three months. I decided to base the tarts on pears as they are locally grown, but to intensify the flavour also incorporated pear juice which I reduced to a syrup, and also used dried pears for their firmer texture and more pronounced flavour. Like most pastry products they are best served warm, and are delicious with thick cream. Tetbury tarts also freeze beautifully.

Tetbury tarts

200g SR flour
50g margarine
50g lard

300 ml pear juice
200g dried pears and apples

100g margarine
100g caster sugar plus 1 tablespoon to glaze
2 eggs
100g SR flour
Duchy Organics Damson jam

- Make the shortcrust pastry, roll out and use to line ten large tartlet tins approximately 10 cm diameter.
- Put baking paper into each pastry base and bake for 10 minutes 180 C Gas 4 (weigh the paper down with pieces of spare pastry).
- Remove the paper and cook for a further 3 minutes.
- Put the pear juice into a saucepan, bring to the boil and reduce by half. Remove 2 tablespoons of the juice for the glaze.
- Cut up the dried fruit into 1 cm pieces.
- Add to the juice and continue to simmer until there is only a little juice left.
- Leave to cool slightly.
- Beat the margarine and sugar together in a bowl, add the eggs and beat well then stir in the flour and fruit mixture.
- Put one tablespoon of the damson jam at the bottom of each cooked pastry case.
- Put a large tablespoon of the pear cake mixture on top of the jam and spread to cover the jam completely.
- Cook for 15 - 20 minutes 200 C Gas 6.
- Mix remaining pear juice with 1 tablespoon of sugar and heat to dissolve.
- Remove the tarts from their tins when they are cooked and brush with the glaze.

I use Bensons pear juice which is a company based in Gloucestershire. They produce apple and pear juices which can be bought from farmers' markets, delicatessens and local farm shops. If you can't find dried pears or pear juice try substituting dried apples and apple juice instead.

Tomato and mozzarella salad uses very simple ingredients but makes a lovely salad for a light lunch. It is wonderful with olive bread or foccacia. Try to buy vine ripened tomatoes (or grow your own) as it makes so much difference to the flavour. Like strawberries, tomatoes are best eaten warm, not chilled, which is why they always taste best as part of a picnic on a hot Summer's day.

Tomato and mozzarella salad

1 buffalo mozzarella
4 large ripe tomatoes
fresh basil
60 ml extra virgin olive oil
freshly ground salt and pepper
black olives

- Drain the mozzarella and cut into slices.
- Cut the tomatoes into slices.
- Arrange the tomatoes and mozzarella on a plate and sprinkle with olive oil.
- Season well with salt and pepper and sprinkle the basil leaves over the top.
- Sprinkle the olives on top.

Instead of the mozzarella, try creamy fresh goats cheese instead.

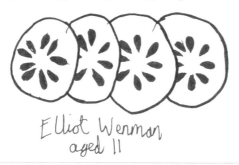

Elliot Wenman
aged 11

91

U pside down pudding can be made with apples, or pears, but is traditionally made with pineapple rings. It is an old fashioned pudding, but my family love it, particularly on a cold winter's day with custard.

Pineapple upside down pudding

1 small tin of pineapple slices in natural juice
4 glace cherries cut in half
100g SR flour
100g soft margarine
100g caster sugar
2 eggs
golden syrup

- Cover the bottom of a 18 cm sandwich tin with a thin layer of golden syrup.
- Arrange the pineapple slices on top and place the cherries in between.
- Put the margarine and sugar in a bowl and cream well together. Add the eggs and beat well.
- Fold in the flour with 1 tablespoon of the pineapple juice.
- Spread the cake mixture carefully over the pineapple.
- Bake for 30 minutes at 180 C Gas 4.
- Place a plate over the top and turn upside down.

Take care when you turn out the pudding as the syrup will be very hot.

V egetable samosas are a good accompaniment to curries but are also lovely as a snack, or as part of a buffet. Traditionally, samosas are fried but this is a lower fat alternative and I find it safer and easier to do with children.

Vegetable samosas

1 pack of filo pastry
1 onion - diced
2 cloves of garlic, crushed
1 teaspoon turmeric
1 teaspoon ground cumin
1 teaspoon garam masala
half a teaspoon chilli powder
1 potato - cooked and diced
1 carrot - cooked and diced
50g frozen peas
vegetable oil

- Put a little oil in a saute pan and add the onion, garlic and spices and cook gently for 5 minutes.
- Add the vegetables and stir well to coat, cook gently and season with salt and pepper. Taste the mixture to check the seasoning and adjust if necessary.
- Allow the mixture to cool.
- Take out two pastry sheets, cut so each piece is approximately 8 x 28 cm and lay one top of another, brush with oil.
- Place a tablespoon of the mixture on the pastry, fold the pastry over in right angled triangles. Seal with water.
- Place on an oiled baking tray and cook for 20 minutes 200 C Gas 6.

93

You can make the samosa filling mixture in advance. Don't try and make them when the filling is still hot because the pastry will be difficult to handle.

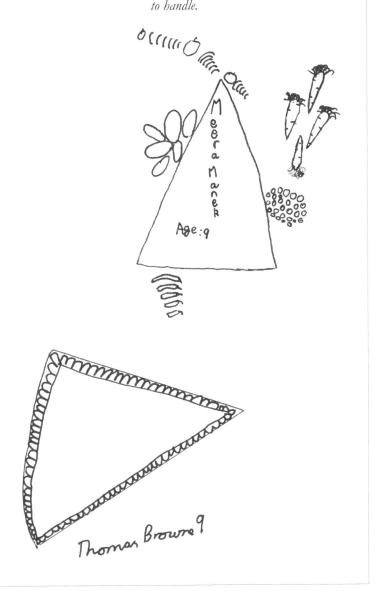

V egetable soup is warming, comforting and a lovely way to eat seasonal vegetables. All the vegetables are high in fibre and full of vitamins. Try to use really fresh vegetables and vary the ingredients according to availability. Fresh herbs really add to the flavour and lentils give the soup a good texture and also add protein to the soup.

Vegetable soup

2 medium potatoes, diced
2 large carrots - finely chopped or grated
1 leek - washed and sliced
1 red pepper, diced
500g carton of passata
1x 300g tin of lentils - drained
1 litre stock or stock cube plus 1 litre water
vegetable oil
salt, pepper and fresh herbs eg thyme
100g smoked streaky bacon, (optional) chopped into small pieces
fresh parsley

- Prepare the potatoes, carrots, leek and red pepper and put in a large saucepan with a little oil and the bacon, if using.
- Saute all the vegetables for 2 or 3 minutes, stirring constantly.
- Add the tin of lentils, passata, stock and fresh herbs, bring to the boil.
- Cover the soup and simmer for 40 - 50 minutes.
- Check the seasoning and add some salt and pepper if needed.
- Adjust the consistency and add a little more water if the soup is too thick.

- Use a hand blender or use a food processor to blend the soup until smooth.
- Pour back into the saucepan, stir in finely chopped fresh parsley and reheat to eat; or leave to cool and divide into smaller portions to freeze.

Vegetable soup is a good way to encourage 'reluctant' vegetable eaters to eat a variety of vegetables. There are so many different vegetables you can use; Try adding some mushrooms or peppers, courgettes, spinach, watercress, celery, parsnips or squash. The perfect accompaniment to home made soup is some lovely fresh bread, and good British cheese.

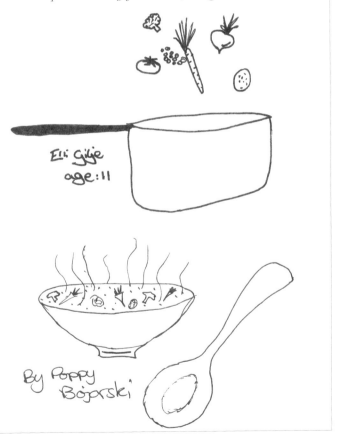

Eli Gilje
age: 11

By Poppy Bojarski

V ictoria sandwich cake is a traditional favourite and it is impossible to buy a cake which will taste as good. Once you have perfected a Victoria sandwich then you can adapt the basic recipe in so many different ways to make birthday cakes, lemon or orange cakes, chocolate or coffee cake.

Victoria sandwich

150g soft margarine or butter
150g caster sugar
150g SR flour
3 large fresh eggs
raspberry jam
sprinkle of icing sugar

- Put margarine and sugar in a mixing bowl and beat together until it is light and creamy (a hand mixer makes this easier).
- Crack the eggs into the mixture and beat well to incorporate lots of air.
- Sieve the flour into the mixture and mix in gently using a metal spoon.
- Cut out two circles of baking paper and place at the bottom of two 18cm sandwich tins.
- Divide the mixture between the two tins.
- Put in a hot oven 200 C Gas 6 for 15 - 20 minutes.
- To test when the cakes are cooked, press the top and it should spring back.
- Turn out onto a cooling rack and leave to cool.
- Sandwich together with jam and sieve a little icing sugar over the top.

To make a chocolate cake replace 25g of flour with cocoa powder.

To decorate

To make some butter cream to fill the cake:
200g icing sugar
100g butter
2 tablespoons water

Optional : 25g cocoa powder, 1 tablespoon of strong coffee, zest of 1 orange or lemon.

For birthday cakes use butter cream in the centre and ice using glace icing or butter cream. Sometimes I use ready to roll icing which is easy to use and always gives a professional looking result.

A nice decoration for chocolate cakes is chocolate leaves: pick some rose leaves, wash them and then dip them or brush some melted plain chocolate on the underside of the leaf. Leave the chocolate to set in the fridge and peel the leaf off. Keep the chocolate leaves cool until needed.

Tim Holland 10

W arm salads are definitely one of my favourite meals in Summer. They are quick to prepare and cook, healthy and so versatile. I do four types regularly, chicken and avocado, black pudding and apple, duck and shallot and my favourite: salade perigourdine. We first had this dish in the beautiful small town of Brantôme in South West France. It was the first time we had eaten a warm salad and loved it. This is our interpretation and is wonderful eaten with good fresh bread.

Black pudding and apple salad serves 3

300g black pudding - sliced
100g smoked bacon - diced
2 coxes apples - sliced
2 cloves of garlic
frisee lettuce or mixed leaves
4 tablespoons olive oil
2 tablespoons of wine vinegar
1 bunch of spring onions
ripe plum tomatoes

- Heat a little olive oil in a saute pan and add the black pudding slices and bacon. Fry gently until almost cooked, then add the apple slices and cook on a high heat to slightly soften and brown the apple.
- Add the tomatoes and chopped spring onions and stir with the other ingredients.
- Place the salad leaves in a large bowl and add the black pudding mixture.
- To the hot pan, add the olive oil, wine vinegar, salt and pepper, and garlic and stir well over heat to deglaze the pan.
- Pour over the salad, toss well and eat immediately.

Salade Perigourdine   serves 3

200g lardons
50g walnuts
4 large free range eggs
2 cloves garlic - crushed
10 ripe small plum tomatoes - cut in half
extra virgin olive oil
mixed salad leaves
wine vinegar
salt and pepper
fresh thyme

- Boil the eggs for 8 minutes, run under cold water and leave to cool slightly.
- Put the salad leaves in a large serving bowl.
- Put one tablespoon of oil into a saute pan and fry the lardons until they are brown.
- Add the tomatoes and garlic, stir and cook quickly until the tomatoes are slightly softened.
- Shell and quarter the eggs and add to the salad with the hot lardon and tomato mixture.
- Into the hot pan, add 4 tablespoons of olive oil, 2 tablespoons of wine vinegar, salt and pepper and a little fresh thyme. Combine over a low heat for 1 minute then pour this dressing over the salad.
- Sprinkle the walnuts over the salad then toss well and eat immediately.

New potatoes added to either salad work well.

W raps are a good alternative to sandwiches and can be filled with interesting and exciting mixtures. They are great for packed lunches and journeys, and children enjoy designing their own fillings. Lots of salad vegetables, fruit, nuts and beans can be incorporated.

Wraps

Smoked salmon and avocado wrap

50g smoked salmon
1 ripe avocado, peeled, stoned and sliced
handful of rocket leaves
2 flat breads or tortillas
juice of half a lemon
ground black pepper

- If you are going to eat the wrap straight away, then warm the flat breads.
- Arrange the slices of avocado and smoked salmon on the flat bread.
- Sprinkle the rocket and lemon juice on top of the salmon and season with freshly ground pepper.
- Turn over the bottom, then roll up the wrap.

This wrap is so lovely for a Summer picnic and is healthy and delicious. The main advantage of wraps rather than sandwiches is that a wrap can contain more filling and the ingredients can be more chunky.

Tuna wrap

100g tuna in oil
half a lemon
mixed salad leaves
spring onions
1 apple - cored and diced
handful of nuts and raisins

- Drain the tuna, mix with all the other ingredients and use to fill a pitta or flat bread.

I use this mixture for filling pitta breads as well as wraps and often make them for packed lunches. There are so many other ingredients that could be added like red pepper, cucumber, kidney beans or grated carrot.

Chicken wrap

cooked chicken
ripe vine tomato
crispy green lettuce
mayonnaise or hummus
fresh basil

- Spread the flat bread with the hummus or mayonnaise. Arrange the chicken, salad and sliced tomato on top, sprinkle with fresh basil and roll up.

This is also good with crisply cooked bacon and avocado.

X

traordinary cake is fun to make and children are amazed to see the chequerboard pattern when they cut the first slice.

Xtraordinary cake

200g margarine
200g caster sugar
200g SR flour
4 eggs
25g cocoa powder
jam

25g cocoa
200g icing sugar
100g butter
2 tablespoons water

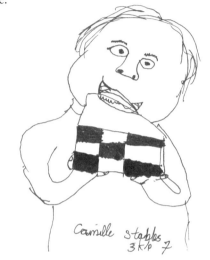

Camille Stables
3 k/p 7

- Put the margarine and sugar into a bowl and cream well together. Beat in the eggs then fold in the flour.
- Put half the mixture into a different bowl and add 25g cocoa powder dissolved in 2 tablespoons of hot water.
- Line the base of two 20 cm sandwich tins with baking paper and put the plain cake mixture in one and the chocolate mixture in the other.
- Cook in a pre-heated oven 200 C Gas 6 for 20 minutes.
- Turn the cakes out onto a cooling rack and leave to cool.
- Cut two circles in each cake (I use a cereal bowl approximately 14 cm and a glass approximately 7 cm and cut around them).

- Remove the second circles from each cake and swap them round, putting jam around the circles before putting them in place.

- You should have one layer which is chocolate, plain, chocolate and another plain, chocolate, plain!
- Sandwich the two cakes together with jam or butter cream.
- Make the chocolate butter cream by creaming the butter, icing sugar, cocoa powder and 2 tablespoons of water together.
- Spread the butter cream on top of the cake and decorate with chocolate flakes or chopped nuts.

This basic recipe can be varied so easily, I have made a super big one with more circles and three layers (I did an orange layer as well) for a birthday cake and covered the whole cake with fondant icing. You could also do a coffee chocolate combination and decorate with chocolate. A ruby orange gives a very good colour to an orange lemon cake and is delicious when sandwiched with good lemon curd. Cover the cake in an orange flavoured glacé icing and decorate with thin strips of orange rind.

X tra special chocolate tart is so delicious and makes a wonderful special occasion dessert. It is important to use good quality cocoa powder and chocolate (70% cocoa solids).

Xtra special chocolate tart

1 pastry case, baked in a 25 cm flan tin
150g butter or margarine
150g plain chocolate-broken up
4 tablespoons cocoa powder
4 eggs
200g caster sugar
3 tablespoons golden syrup
3 tablespoons soured cream

- Place the butter, chocolate and cocoa powder over a pan of simmering water and allow to melt slowly, stirring occasionally.
- In another bowl beat the eggs and sugar together until light and creamy.
- Add the golden syrup and soured cream.
- Stir the chocolate mixture into this mixture and mix well.
- Pour the mixture into the cooked pastry case.
- Bake for 45 minutes 160 C Gas 3.
- Remove from oven and leave to cool.

This dessert is best eaten warm and is delicious with vanilla ice cream.

Yule log is something children love to make at Christmas and is something they can do with very little help - if you are prepared to have a slightly sticky kitchen afterwards!

Yule log

1 large chocolate swiss roll
125g icing sugar
25g cocoa powder
75g butter or margarine - softened
2 tablespoons of water

Icing sugar to sieve on top
Christmas cake decorations

- Place the swiss roll on a cake board. If it is too long cut a little off at an angle and place it on the side as a branch.
- Put the icing sugar, cocoa, softened butter and water in a bowl and beat well together until it is smooth and creamy.
- Check the consistency of the butter icing. If it is too stiff, add another tablespoon of water. If it is too runny add some more icing sugar.
- Use a knife to spread the butter icing all over the swiss roll to cover it completely.
- Use a fork to make your log look realistic.
- Sprinkle over a little icing sugar and arrange your Christmas decorations on top.

Enjoy straight away or freeze until needed.

Yoghurt is such a useful ingredient and I had to include this recipe because it was the first recipe I ever cooked for my husband. I served it with steak, jacket potato, and a side salad and he always remembered it.

Yoghurt and aubergine casserole

2 large aubergines - sliced
1 large onion - thinly sliced
2 garlic cloves - crushed
vegetable oil
500g carton of passatta
1 tablespoon of tomato puree
half a teaspoon of dried basil
half a teaspoon of sugar
salt and freshly ground pepper
1 small carton of natural yoghurt
50g freshly grated parmesan
25g fresh breadcrumbs

- Fry the aubergine slices, a few at a time, in a little oil (if you use a non stick pan, less oil will be needed). Drain on kitchen paper.
- Fry the onion gently until soft then add the garlic, the passatta, tomato puree, basil, sugar, salt and pepper. Bring to the boil and reduce slightly.
- Layer the aubergine slices with the tomato sauce and yoghurt, finishing with a layer of aubergine. Sprinkle the top with parmesan and breadcrumbs.
- Bake for 30 minutes 180 C Gas 4.

This is a good vegetarian dish or as an accompaniment to roast lamb or chicken.

Z esty lemon pudding is creamy and comforting. It separates into two layers when it is cooked and should be quite tangy, so the balance between the lemon and sugar is quite important. This recipe serves 6, but if you have any left it is still very good the next day.

Zesty lemon pudding

100g margarine or butter
200g caster sugar
rind and juice of 3 lemons
4 large eggs - separated
100g SR flour
500 ml milk

- Put the margarine, sugar and lemon rind in a bowl and cream together.
- Add the egg yolks and beat well (a hand mixer makes this easier).
- Add the flour, milk and lemon juice and beat well.
- In a clean bowl, whisk the egg whites until stiff (if you use the hand mixer make sure the beaters are very clean).
- Fold the egg whites into the lemon mixture until thoroughly combined.
- Pour the mixture into a greased dish approximately 25 cm x 30 cm.
- Cook in a pre-heated oven 180 C Gas 4 for 45 minutes (or slightly longer if you are using a deeper dish).
- This pudding is nicest eaten warm.

This pudding is also really delicious with oranges.

Celebrity Specials

Go wild in the kitchen Love

Antony Worrall Thompson

All the best

Curtis Stone

Happy Cooking!

Nick Nairn

Wishing you all many years of Happy Cooking! With best Wishes

Gary Rhodes

With love, luck & happiness

Paul Da Costa-Greaves

Rick Stein

Cook with your children & make it fun. With my Best Wishes

JW Burton-Race

109

Rick Stein's Crab Pasties with Leek and Saffron makes 6

Ingredients
900g/2lb chilled fresh puff pastry
½ tsp saffron strands
2 tsp hot water
350g/12oz white crab meat
75g/3oz brown crab meat
225g/8oz leeks, thinly sliced
50g/2oz fresh white breadcrumbs
1 tsp salt
10 turns of the white pepper mill
25g/1oz butter, melted

- Preheat the oven to 200 C 400 F Gas 6.
- Divide the pastry into 6 pieces. Roll out each piece on a lightly floured surface and cut into a 19cm / 7½in circle.
- For the filling, soak the saffron in the hot water for 5 minutes. Put the white and brown crab meat, leeks, breadcrumbs, salt and pepper into a bowl and stir together until well mixed.
- Crush the saffron a little into the water to release the colour and flavour, then stir it into the melted butter. Now stir this into the rest of the filling ingredients.
- Divide the filling mixture between the pastry circles. Brush the edge of one half with a little water, bring both sides together over the top of the filling and pinch together well to seal.
- Crimp the edge of each pasty decoratively between your fingers, transfer to a lightly greased baking sheet and bake for 35 minutes, until golden brown. Serve hot or cold.

Ainsley's Fruity Pork Fillets with Root Puree

For the Mash...
8oz parsnips, cubed
8oz floury potatoes, cubed
3 - 4 tablespoons milk
1½ oz butter
salt and freshly ground black pepper

For the pork...
8oz tenderloin pork fillet, cut into ½ inch slices
1 tablespoon flour, seasoned with salt and pepper
2oz butter
8 ready to eat prunes soaked for at least thirty minutes in dry white wine
1 tablespoon of cranberry or redcurrant jelly
5 fl oz of double cream
juice of ½ lemon
salt and pepper

- Cook parsnips and potatoes in a large pan of boiling, salted water for 10 - 12 minutes until tender. Dust the pork with the seasoned flour. Heat half the butter in a large frying pan and when foaming, cook the pork for 1 - 2 minutes on each side. Remove and set aside.
- Strain the wine into a hot pan and bring to the boil. Stir in the redcurrant jelly and cook for a further two minutes, until melted. Add the cream, prunes and pork, season to taste and gently simmer until the pork is cooked through.

- Drain the root vegetables and mash well. Add the milk and remaining butter and whizz with an electric hand whisk until smooth and puréed. Season to taste. Squeeze a little lemon juice into the pork pan and check the seasoning. Pile the mash on to serving plates and spoon over the pork mixture.
- Serve with green beans.

Spinach and roasted red pepper tortilla
Antony Worrall Thompson

A lovely dish for lunch. Quick, colourful, tasty and it's good for you.

Serves 4 - 6
450 ml (16 fl oz) olive oil
6 medium potatoes, peeled and cut into 1/6 in (4 mm) slices
2 large onions, peeled, 1 thinly sliced, chopped
450g (1lb) spinach, washed, thick stems removed
4 roasted peppers, 2 red and 2 yellow, chopped into slices
3 tablespoons extra virgin olive oil
2 cloves garlic, peeled and crushed
2 tablespoons finely chopped parsley and thyme
coarse salt and freshly ground black pepper
a pinch of paprika
6 free-range eggs, beaten with 4 tablespoons double cream

- Heat the olive oil in a deep frying pan. Add the potatoes alternating in layers with thinly sliced onion. Cook gently, covered, until the potatoes are just tender (they should remain separate, but not brown).
- Meanwhile, place the greens in salted boiling water for 15 minutes with 1 tablespoon of the extra virgin olive oil. Drain and chop coarsely.
- In a frying pan, heat the remaining extra virgin olive oil. Fry the chopped onion until wilted, then add the greens and the peppers and continue cooking for a further 8 minutes. Add the garlic, parsley, and thyme, salt, pepper and paprika.

- When the potatoes are cooked, drain them of excess oil, and mix with the greens. Transfer this mixture to a shallow non-stick frying pan that will go in the oven. The dish may be made in advance to this point.
- Preheat the oven to 190°C 375°F Gas 5. Pour the eggs and cream over the pan, shake and place in the oven for 15 minutes or until the eggs have set. Allow to cool, turn out on to a plate and dribble with extra virgin olive oil.

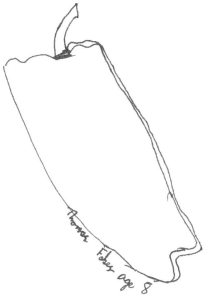

Thomas Beasley Age: 10

Vegetable Tagine
Antony Worrall Thompson

A great dinner dish incorporating vegetables and spices without blowing your head off!

Serves 4

2 tablespoons olive oil
450g (1lb) onion, half grated and half cut into chunky dice
half a head of garlic, peeled and crushed with salt
half a tablespoon ground ginger
half a teaspoon ground black pepper
half a teaspoon ground cinnamon
175g (6oz) dried apricots, soaked in a little water
85g (3oz) flaked almonds
55g (2oz) sultanas, raisins
1 tablespoon liquid honey
600ml (1 pint) tomato juice
600ml (1 pint) vegetable stock
280g (10 oz) potatoes, peeled and cut into 1 inch chunks
2 green peppers, de-seeded and cut into 1 inch chunks
280g (10 oz) pumpkin, peeled, deseeded and cut into 1 inch chunks
1 x 400g (14 oz) tin chickpeas, drained and rinsed
1 x 400g (14 oz) tin chopped tomatoes
280g (10 oz) cauliflower florets
2 large courgettes, cut into 1 inch chunks
280g (10 oz) fresh peas
25g (1 oz) chopped coriander
salt

- In a large ovenproof casserole dish heat the olive oil, when hot add onions, garlic and spices. Gently cook until the onions are soft and translucent. Be careful not to brown.

- Add the apricots and their soaking water, the almonds, raisins/sultanas, honey, tomato juice and vegetable stock. Bring to the boil, reduce the heat and allow to simmer until the sauce has reduced by half.
- Add the vegetables in order of cooking time, start with the potatoes and green peppers and gently cook for approximately 12 minutes then add the pumpkin, tinned tomatoes and chickpeas. Cook for 8 minutes then add the courgettes, cauliflower florets, and the fresh peas. Continue to cook until all the vegetables are tender, about a further 10 minutes. Sprinkle with coriander and serve immediately. Season to taste. Serve with couscous.

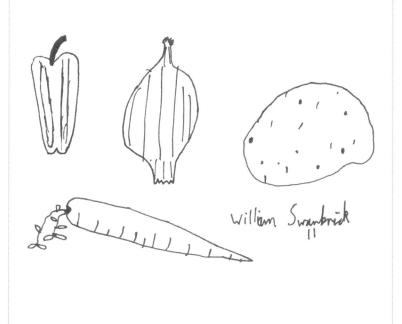

William Swanbrick
11

Chicken Casserole with Coriander Dumplings
Gordon Ramsay
Serves 12

12 boned chicken thighs
1 litre chicken stock
4 sticks of celery washed and sliced
2 leeks white only finely chopped
4 spring onions finely sliced
4 carrots peeled and chopped
2 parsnips peeled and chopped
1 celeriac peeled and finely diced
1 bay leaf
2 sprig of thyme
salt and freshly ground pepper
250g plain flour
100g suet
3 tablespoon chopped fresh coriander

- Place the chicken in a large stock pot or saucepan. Add the stock and bring to the boil. Add the chopped vegetables, bring the stock back to the boil, lower the heat, add the herbs and season well. Simmer for 2 - 3 hours until the chicken is tender. Remove from the heat and allow to cool. This can be done a day in advance.
- Skim any fat from the surface of the stock, then lift out the chicken pieces and remove and discard the skin and break into bite sized pieces. Check the seasoning and return the meat to the pan.

- In a large mixing bowl mix together the flour suet and coriander. Add enough cold water to form a soft dough. Form into small dumplings. Bring the casserole to the boil and then drop in the dumplings. Poach for 10 - 15 minutes or until doubled in size and fluffy.
- Serve immediately.

Claire Fabes 10

Gabriel Drewett

I love cooking.....

I love cooking mince pies because I love getting messy when I make the dough.

Alice
5A

I like cooking because I like eating what I have made and sharing it with my family. I also like it because it is relaxing and fun!

I like cooking because ....

I like cooking because on a sunday I go to my nans. I like to help with the fruit salad with my nans help! I like to cut the strawberries !!

Alexandra Burdass
age 10

Emma. Devlin
Cooking is fun because there is loads of ingredients and it is messy and nice to do it with your parents.

Callum Horn 10

I like cooking because it's fun and because it's nice when my mum has time toas it with me.

Flora McGivan
age 11

I love cooking because I love starting with only a few ingredients and ending up with a delicious end product.

Elliot Wenman
aged 11

I Like cooRing Because I Like food!
By Leah Ratcliffe Age 8

I like shaping the fresh warm dough because it smells really good!

Hugo Glass, age 10

I like cooking because it is nice to know that you are eating something you have made your self.

Lydia Jones
age 11

I love cooking because,

When my nan asked if I wanted a cake I said yes and can I help and I loved it it was really great. From this day on I love cooking

Kieran Ratcliff
5A

I like cooking because I get mucky and I like spending time with my family.

Lucy Wray 5A

I love cooking because I like shaping the dough and I love making lemon cake !

Sam Boren-Reast Age: 11

I like cooking because I get to have a good chat whith my Mum.

Tom

I love making food at home because I can't wait to try it when it's cooked and I also like being by the hot aga.

Anastasia Robinson
age 10

Chandlings Manor School

I love cooking because I loved getting my hands all gewy! and I loved cooking the bread it tased delicous!

By Imogen. Reid   age 8

I love cooking lots of things especially deserts, I also love cooking things because I can try lots of different food especially vegetables because my mum is allways complaining because I'm not that keen on vegetables but I definetely want to like them!

Cass cassidy 11

I love cooking because I love getting my hands messy! I especially like making pancakes and fliping them.

Caroline Viney, age 10

I love cooking for special occasions because when everyone eats it, it is nice to know that you made it.

Alice Telger
age 10

I love eating what I have made because I can decide what I make and make sure I like it. I like making chocolate cake because it always smells nice when it is in the oven.

by Nathan Jayne
age 10

I love cooking because it is fun and really exciting making lots of different things. My favourite thing is making cakes with my Nanny.

Grace I-S
5R.

I love eating fresh pasta because its slimey

william Bishop aged 10

Index
Page

Sausage and bean casserole	75-76
Tagliatelle with baby vegetables	85-86
Yoghurt and aubergine casserole	107

Biscuits

Chocolate chip cookies	25
Chocolate oaties	57
Easter biscuits	29
Shortbread	74
Pudsey bear biscuits	66
Muesli bars	53
Gingerbread men	35

Cakes

Apple muffins	5
Apricot loaf	8
Banana and nut loaf	11
Chris's Chocolate cake	21-22
Date and walnut cake	26
Easter nests	30
Fairy cakes	31-32
Nutty date squares	56
Parkin	62
Pain au raisin	60
Queen cakes	67
Raspberry muffins	54
Scones	73
Swiss roll	79-80
Teabread	83
Tetbury tarts	89-90
Victoria sandwich	97-98
Xtraordinary cake	103-104
Yule log	106

Bread
Bread rolls	16
Hot cross buns	37-38
Focaccia	33
Chelsea buns	19-20

Puddings
Apple crumble	6
Apple cake	4
Bread and butter pudding	15
Christmas pudding	23-24
Fresh fruit salad	34
Jelly cups	41
Lemon meringue pie	47-48
Meringues	51
Mince pies	52
Orange pudding	59
Pineapple upside down pudding	92
Plum ice cream	40
Pancakes	61
Rhubarb fool	71
Summer pudding	82
Short crust pastry	64
Tarte au pomme	87
Tartes aux fruits	88
Xtra special chocolate tart	105
Zesty lemon pudding	108

Drinks
Caribbean fruit punch	17
Lemonade	49
Smoothies	81

Celebrity specials

Ainsley Harriot :
Fruity pork fillets with root puree   111-112

Rick Stein:
Rick Steins Crab Pasties with Leek and   110
Saffron

Antony Worrall Thompson :
Spinach and roasted red pepper tortilla   113-114
Vegetable tagine   115-116

Gordon Ramsay:
Chicken Casserole with Coriander   117-118
Dumplings

Notes

_____

_____

_____

_____

_____

_____

_____

_____

_____

_____

_____

_____

Notes

Notes

_____

_____

_____

_____

_____

_____

_____

_____

_____

_____

_____

_____

Acknowledgments

Thank you so much, Laura for all your hard work, and for understanding why this book means a lot to me. Thank you Emma and Anne for taking the time to proof read all the recipes with such care and attention. Special thanks to Judy, for making it possible for me to teach Food at Chandlings, and for the total support you always give me, professionally and personally.

A huge thank you to all the children at Chandlings who made me want to write this book, your enthusiasm and pleasure in cooking is wonderful, and is the reason I love my job.

Thank you to Shaun and all the staff at Chandlings for your ideas, friendship, and sense of humour.

Huge thanks to Roger, Robin and Richard and everyone at Information Press for your support, time and for printing this book in memory of Chris.

Thank you also to Blenheim Colour, Brittannia Print Finishers, and Robert Horne Paper Company all of whom gave their services to support this project and raise money for Cancer research in Chris' memory.

Thank you to Mum for encouraging my brothers and me to cook when we were little, and for not minding the mess we made.

Thank you to my lovely children Harriet and Robert, who have enthusiastically sampled almost every recipe in this book! You are just amazing.

Lastly, thank you to Chris, we started this together and I finished it for you.